THE BUTTERFLY
AND THE STONE

A son. A father.
God's love on a prodigal journey.

DAN N. MAYHEW

ISBN-10: 1461113903
ISBN-13: 978-1461113904

DEDICATION

For Jody, Jenna, Corrie and Caleb,

my traveling companions.

For the hundreds who have prayed for us on the journey.

And in memory of

Army Staff Sgt. David J. Weisenburg

whose life and friendship remains a gift to us all.

CONTENTS

Preface   iii

1   Apprehension   1

2   Judgment   5

3   Doubt   9

4   Letting Go   13

5   Identity   17

6   Regret   21

7   Uniqueness   25

8   Grace   29

9   Listening   33

10   Devotion   37

11   Trust   41

12   Faith   45

13   Grief   49

14   Honor   53

15   Shame   57

16	Yearning	61
17	Generations	65
18	Wrath	69
19	Terror	73
20	Seeking	77
21	Endurance	81
22	Hope	85
23	Promise	89
24	Idols	93
25	Despair	97
26	Grace Upon Grace	101
27	Loss	105
28	Addiction	109
29	Wounds	113

Jesus told them this story...

A man had two sons. The younger son told his father, "I want my share of your estate now, instead of waiting until you die."

So his father agreed to divide his wealth between his sons. A few days later this younger son packed all his belongings and took a trip to a distant land, and there he wasted all his money on wild living. About the time his money ran out, a great famine swept over the land, and he began to starve. He persuaded a local farmer to hire him to feed his pigs. The boy became so hungry that even the pods he was feeding the pigs looked good to him. But no one gave him anything.

When he finally came to his senses, he said to himself, "At home even the hired men have food enough to spare, and here I am, dying of hunger! I will go home to my father and say, 'Father, I have sinned against both heaven and you, and I am no longer worthy of being called your son. Please take me on as a hired man.'"

So he returned home to his father. And while he was still a long distance away, his father saw him coming. Filled with love and compassion, he ran to his son, embraced him, and kissed him. His son said to him, "Father, I have sinned against both heaven and you, and I am no longer worthy of being called your son."

But his father said to the servants, "Quick! Bring the finest robe in the house and put it on him. Get a ring for his finger, and sandals for his feet. And kill the calf we have been fattening in the pen. We must celebrate with a feast, for this son of mine was dead and has now returned to life. He was lost, but now he is found."

~Luke 15: 11-24 (NLT)

i

PREFACE

Hope is a butterfly,

Fear is a stone,

As a father waits

For his son to come home.

I think of the story Jesus told about the prodigal son. In the story, the wanderer comes home. He is seen from afar and his father runs to meet him and there is a celebration.

The great storm is over.

But prodigal journeys are rarely like that, rarely so resolute. They are like a long story with multiple climactic moments that eventually subside in a tedious, tentative denouement. You pause at the last page uncertain whether more is yet to be written.

Or they are like a play with one crisis after another sprinkled unexpectedly throughout. And then it ends abruptly, and without finality—an empty stage and the audience left shifting uneasily in their seats waiting for the house lights to come up. They wonder if they should leave or wait for another scene, or if they should stand with nervous applause.

Yet, on this prodigal journey I have discovered a truth so deep that I can scarcely accept it. I resist it because it stands against what I have come to believe. I resist it because, binding my heart like a cable, is a lie: I am too broken, too wicked and resistant to the ways of righteousness; too tainted with stubborn sin to be anything more to God than a disappointment, and an object of loathing. No holy God would stand for me.

And then I remember Benjamin, my only son. I remember each fearful failure and experience the resentment over each rebellious incident; sense the old pain and anger. Yet, out of that crucible of rejection comes, not hatred, but compassion. Not loathing, but love.

How can that be? I love him. Even now, I would die for him. Against all sense, I love my son. And therein lies the deepest truth of the prodigal journey: If I, with all my faults, know how to give good gifts to my children, how much more will my Father in heaven give good things to me if I would but ask (Matthew 7:11).

This book is not a memorial, not an epitaph. My son, after all, is alive. This is a chronicle of hurts, and a journal of hopes; a diary of fears and a canon of dreams. It is a journey ongoing, to a destination uncertain. It is a narrative of waywardness and the lessons that come from it. Moreover, it is not a devotional, nor a book of advice on parenting. It is a book of questions that hunger for answers; or, perhaps, of encouragement—the hopeful sound of a distant voice in the darkest night that says you are not alone. At the heart, it is the story of God and me— and all His rebellious sons; of the Father and His prodigal race, as seen in the dark mirror of earthly fatherhood.

The challenge will be to find the hope in the story when the end seems anything but certain. Hope in the midst of waywardness is not certainty, only cautious, even desperate, optimism. That's what love does to you. It makes it impossible to give up even when you so desperately want to, because to give up means amputation, like the mountain climber whose arm became hopelessly lodged in the rocks. Finally, in desperation he sawed off his own arm to get free.

Rather hack off an arm or a leg than to abandon my son, to amputate hope.

And that is the first lesson I learned from my son: love never fails, it cannot give up. It is, by definition, stubborn and furious. And if I can see such foolish, tenacious and furious love in my own heart then it is a reflection of the furious love of God and the iron grip of grace on me, my Father's wayward son.

Wendell Berry, in his novel, Jayber Crow, wrote:

If God loved the world even before the event at Bethlehem, that meant He loved it as it was, with all its faults. That would be Hell itself, in part. He would be like a father with a wayward child, whom He can't help and can't forget. But it would be even worse than that, for He would also know the wayward child and the course of its waywardness and its suffering. That His love contains all the world does not show that the world does not matter, or that He and we do not suffer it unto death; it shows that the world is Hell only in part. But His love can contain it only by compassion and mercy, which, if not Hell entirely, would be at least a crucifixion. [1]

Desperate love leads to desperate ends. It invites us to the edge of reason and bids us leap. I learned that such love cannot simply be amputated without fundamentally changing the amputee. Were it an arm or a leg I could get by. But to deny love would leave me in a netherworld, alive but numb and indifferent, not just feeling hopeless but being without it utterly.

No, desperate love cannot give up and settle for a dismal half-death. Love for a wayward son demands it all.

I understand my Father. He hasn't given up on me. He can't. His love persists beyond reason because that is love by definition, and that is how I came to learn God's name. Jayber Crow continues:

I imagined that the right name [for God] might be Father, and I imagined all that that name would imply: the love, the compassion, the taking offense, the disappointment, the anger, the bearing of wounds, the weeping of tears, the forgiveness, the suffering unto death. If love could force my own thoughts over the edge of the world and out of time, then could I not see how even divine omnipotence might by the force of its own love be swayed down into the world? Could I not see how it might, because it could know its creatures only by compassion, put on mortal flesh, become a man, and walk among us, assume our nature and our fate, suffer our faults and our death? [2]

It's been fifteen years on the prodigal journey. When it began—junior high—love was already there. Then began offense, disappointments, the bearing of wounds, anger, and the weeping of tears. Yet, love remains, like a chrysalis among stones. It appears vulnerable—doomed. But it remains because love is born in the Father-heart of God, and so it is written:

[Love] bears all things, believes all things, hopes all things, endures all things. Love never ends. And now these three remain: faith, hope, and love. But the greatest of these is love. [3]

---

1 Jayber Crow (Washington D.C.: Counterpoint, 2000), p. 251.

2 Ibid, p. 251-252.

3 1 Corinthians 13:13

(1) APPREHENSION

It must have been a Monday—Ben's ninth grade year. We had our fingers crossed. Junior high had been a dubious adventure so high school was a make-or-break proposition. Nothing serious had happened in Junior high, just what you might expect from a rambunctious 7th grader, but with numerous disciplinary issues on his record we thought it might be best to school him at home for 8th grade.

Now, we were well into his freshman year.

"OK, I'll see you Thursday," I was saying. "I'll be spending some time with the guys down at the coast."

"Going to hang out with the Bible thumpers, huh?" he said.

Bible thumpers? Something jabbed at my insides. Bible thumpers? Where did that come from? I worked with pastors on occasion—three or four times a year—facilitating prayer gatherings, but our personal church life looked quite untraditional. We met in homes, not in a traditional church meeting hall; moreover, I couldn't remember ever thumping a bible in the style of some fiery fundamentalist. That was a whole different world than ours, if such a world existed at all.

I pulled up to the school. "Have a great week," I said. "Love ya."

"I love you, too." He popped open the car door and got out, and then, "have a good time with the Bible thumpers!" And he turned and strode away.

There was something about his remarks that troubled me. I realized that there were new influences in his life and that he was embracing them—trying them on. I told myself that was normal. Teens are supposed to do that. An adolescent has to look beyond his home world and into the universe. It is all part of growing up.

But it wouldn't stop there. It didn't really start there, either. In truth, I had been apprehensive for months, and the coming weeks would only confirm my suspicions that he had taken up smoking. A girl offered him a cigarette and he, like so many others, took that easy ticket into a group. I cringed. Having been a high school teacher for several years I knew what went along with that ticket: an open invitation to "just go hang out," meaning to stand around and smoke; it meant a free pass to somebody's party and beer. It would mean that his only friends would be others who smoked and did the things that kids who also took that easy ticket frequently did. It meant that pot and often other drugs were going to be within his reach. And it meant that the kids who chose not to smoke—didn't feel the need for the easy ticket—would not be within Ben's circle of friends.

We had always tried to encourage the kids to be active so they would have a positive peer group. We did soccer with the girls, baseball with Ben. But the American pastime was glacially slow for him; so then we tried wrestling, then karate. Nothing stuck, and the apprehension grew. We felt like we were in a car rolling down a hill with no brakes and only limited steering. Desperation began to take over. I even tried getting him into Boy Scouts—catastrophe. The other boys knew what Ben was intending to become and weren't buying it. The irony was that Jon, who was to become Ben's best friend—one of the band of brothers who would go with him to Iraq—was in that very group. Ben and Jon would not become friends until later.

So, the spiral continued and I, the father, could do nothing, at least nothing that helped—all futile efforts.

What made it so difficult was that window into adolescent life, those years I had spent in the high school classroom watching students on the downward spiral; watching some of them take the easy ticket to rebellion and underachievement, the ticket to ride on the Prodigal Railway. I had gotten a rare glimpse of my son's future.

As I pause, now, to consider those days I think of my heavenly father who had—who has—more than a glimpse my future. Jayber Crow's observations about the love of God are spot on: He would be like a father with a wayward child, whom He can't help and can't forget. But it would be even worse than that, for He would also know the wayward child and the course of its waywardness and its suffering.

The old hymn says, "O, what peace we often forfeit. O, what needless pain we bear..." I think of all the bruises and sorrows of my own prodigal journey. If only I had been more attentive to the Father! The journey would have been so different.

It would have. But the walk of a follower of Jesus is not laid to what might have been. It begins with what is, and only from there does it lead to destiny. That is what I have to remember about my own son. What might have been...ought to have been...should have been, does not matter. What can and will be is what matters because his future, indeed my future, is in the hands of the Father. Father has entrusted a future to both of us—all of us. Now, just as on that day in his freshman year, we are two prodigals on a journey together.

(2) JUDGMENT

"He does not respect you."

They were the words of a friend speaking of my young son. As I recall, we were standing in the kitchen and my friend was at our sink rinsing some dishes, helping straighten up after a meeting at our house. The words cut deep and I bled softly for three days. They echoed in my silent drive to the river that afternoon and stung for the hour or so that I sat watching the boats. They spoke into my waking moments of reflection when my mind would wander from the immediate task. Eventually, I put them behind me, but for three days I ached.

Some of the time I was angry: "Who does he think he is, anyway?" Anger is one way of bleeding.

As often as anger came despair: "He's right. Even others notice." Despair bleeds.

I'm sure he thought it was the right thing to do. He probably had waited for the "right moment" to point out what he should have known was painfully obvious to me. I don't know what incident prompted the remark or anything he, or I, said after it, only that he felt compelled to speak about our family. He had probably thought about it and discussed his thoughts with his wife. They had probably agreed that something should be said about Ben's behavior, but that they should wait for "an opening."

Why do I think that? Because that is what I have done in years past, before my hands were forced to grip the fiery throttle of experience.

I remember sitting in the conference room of a mega-church of which I was a part, discussing which of the men in

5

the congregation should be invited to become an elder. We all sat around the table considering a list of names. Lowell was on the list. He was a good man. Compassionate. Conscientious. Wise. One of the elders had told him he was being considered. Later, we invited him to a meeting to talk about the matter. We asked him questions about doctrine, about his testimony of faith, and eventually, about Aaron, his eighth-grade son.

Aaron was rowdy. He played the part of the young rebel. Some suspected he was smoking. And didn't the bible say an elder should have children under control—rule his household well?

Lowell sat unmoving, but not unmoved, at the head of the conference table. His face was expressionless. "I didn't ask to be an elder," he said. "You asked me."

I don't remember much more of the meeting. I don't believe we made him an elder. I don't know what happened to Aaron, either. I do know we judged Lowell...just as I quietly went on judging a number of parents over the years before Ben became our prodigal. Now, it occurs to me that Lowell, of all of us who sat at that table, may have been the most qualified for eldership. Who among us understood the pain of sin better than he? Which of us knew the sorrow of rejected counsel; the pain that emerges from rebellion, the desperation of love for the rebel? In short, which of us understood the Father heart of God better than he?

Instead, we presumed that his son's behavior was evidence that Lowell himself was guilty of some hidden failure, that all was not as it seemed in his life and family. Aaron was the smoking gun that we leveled at Lowell's heart and fired.

Years later Jody and I would be invited into our living room by a young couple, ten years married and childless, who had come to live with us. They said they wanted to talk with us about something. We all sat uneasily for a few moments. Finally, the young man confessed it was about Benjamin. They were concerned for what sin must have been in our family for him to behave as he did.

There it was. That which had remained unspoken by them, and apparently by others, was in the light. Sin. Failure. If we had been better parents—good parents—would our son be rebellious and sullen? Surely not. Diligent parents will inherit the blessing of obedient children. The slackers, the workaholics, the alcoholics, the indifferent, intolerant and impatient will inherit the wind.

I used to think like that. I was among the suspicious observers of families torn by rebellion. I would wonder what that family had really been like behind closed doors and out of sight. What sin must have been hidden there?

Jesus said, *Do not judge others, and you will not be judged. For you will be treated as you treat others. The standard you use in judging is the standard by which you will be judged.*

I don't for an instant think that God has visited judgment on me because of my ignorant judgment of others. If I have learned anything on the prodigal journey, I have learned that my Father is compassionate and shares my sorrow, shame and desperation. He, too, understands anguish over a child who uses his freedom for self-destruction. He understands that even in a garden of provision and nurture and love a prodigal may appear.

I think Lowell knew that. Now, I know it, too.

(3) DOUBT

Dear Ben-

Sometimes it's tough to be able to express myself, so I thought I'd try in a way that seems to work for me. Writing comes naturally, I guess.

I wanted to let you know that I've noticed you growing lately—not just physically, although you're doing that, too. But lately you've been making some hard decisions. Taking classes at the community college was a hard choice, but you've done it and I think the choices are good.

I know that entering into this new school world is a little intimidating. You've not felt as though you could succeed in that environment so you haven't been real anxious to take the risk, but you have and I'm proud that you did. I am praying that you keep yourself committed to what lies ahead. I am confident that if you give yourself a chance to succeed—I mean take the risk—that you will. Once that happens your whole viewpoint will change. The good news is that I know you can do it. The bad news is I'm not sure you do! Who knows? Maybe you'll find something that will challenge and delight you. As long as you have to work to make money, you might as well find something you love. If you don't mind working in a warehouse or doing landscaping that's fine, but if they're just "for the money" you may as well find something

9

that not only pays, but that fascinates and brings you joy and satisfaction.

I also know that it was tough to take on a second job. My guess is that you won't have to work the night shift too long. His turnover at the gym is high. You'll be able to switch to days soon, I bet.

I also want to thank you for letting me share briefly in your date tonight. I know it's selfish, but I like to watch as you do stuff like that. It's a part of life as a dad that I missed. Truthfully, I wasn't ready for the school years to be over. When you got done with all that so soon, I was caught off balance. School was a world that was yours, but that I could peek into and share a bit as you made your way to freedom and maturity. Anyhow, it was cool to see you head off to a dance (looking pretty studly, I might add!). Strange how dumb stuff like that is important to old folks, huh?

Hope you had a great time. Even if you didn't it was cool to watch you try. Too bad I couldn't have seen your "lady." You probably made a great couple.

Well that's all for now. I just wanted you to know that I am very encouraged about you and your choices right now. Keep up the good work.

Dad

Yet another letter found on the hard-drive. Did I give it to him? I don't remember. Probably. It was the desperate or angry ones I usually filed away or deleted.

The occasion was the day after a high school dance. He had dropped out a year or two before, so it was, as I recall, a date with one of his classmates who had remained in school. It was a wistful moment for me. It was a chance to play a game of "what might have been."

His childhood had ended so abruptly! He had discarded it and moved on to a darker world, a place in which parents are not welcome. No sporting events to go watch. No dances to see him off to. No back-to-school nights. No commencement. After a dozen fruitless meetings with the assistant principal we had to give the teachers a break and release him from school. It all just ended. In its place were accumulating months of ambiguity. It had become a game with a whole new set of rules.

As I re-read the letter the feelings come back: I know I'm not supposed to judge and cajole, I'm supposed to be encouraging and supportive. I don't want my relationship with him to be summed up in, why did ya? why don't ya? would ya? couldn't ya? shouldn't ya? will ya? won't ya? are ya? aren't ya...I was constantly looking for the things I could affirm and for the right things to say that wouldn't drive him further away. And in the middle of it all I was trying to grab a little more of the joy of parenting that I wasn't ready to let go of.

That's what I see in the letter. A desperate attempt to stay positive, hoping that encouragement would nudge him to success and self-respect. That's what the experts say to do, isn't it? Be affirming. Be encouraging. Don't nag and belittle. Don't dwell on the failures and the negatives. Put a 'happy face' sticker on everything. Don't mark his papers—or his life—with red ink. Every kid's life should have scrawled in the margins: GOOD JOB!!

Do that and your child will thrive.

Maybe it was too little, too late. He dropped out of community college and never started the job at the gym. Or maybe encouragement—being interested and genuinely loving—worked backwards in our family. Or maybe he wasn't convinced that I was being honest with him; that I really did believe that he had what it takes.

But I did. I believed every word...and still do.

How much of God's love do I doubt? Is that what makes me a prodigal? Not being able to accept that God's mercy can extend even to me? Does the prodigal heart automatically convert even the truth into a lie? God doesn't really love me. He hasn't forgiven me. He knows the truth: I am a loser...

Perhaps that is why sometimes the truth does not set us free, because though it is true, we must also believe that it is true. That is perhaps the hardest thing for the prodigal to do.

(4) LETTING GO

"Ephraim is given to idols, leave him alone."
~Hosea 4:17

Dear Ben-

You'll get this after I've left. Funny how these "crisis situations" always seem to precede a time when I have to leave. Anyhow, I'm sorry to have to be gone.

I am writing to let you know that I am not mad at you. I'm feeling a bit depressed, but I guess that's to be expected. We just couldn't figure out anything else to do. Our options were gone. We've suggested, asked, threatened, and reasoned in hopes that you'd give up certain behaviors, but we realize now that those things will never work. You will live according to your standards and not ours. You're an adult, so that's what you need to do, I guess.

Your long range options as I see them are to "get treatment" if you know in your heart that you've got a problem. Or, you can go full time military. That's a possibility that you've been considering anyhow. You could also "go away to school." You have the financial help now to do that, and you could live in the dorms like your sisters and I did. The only thing that I worry about is the dorm life has been the same for the last 100 years and it often includes a lot of drinking and partying. I'm not sure that's the best for you under the circumstances.

Short term, you'll need to couch surf with some friends for a while until you get some money together. Barring that, you have some other options you may not have thought about...I have no doubt you'll come out all right. You usually get resourceful when you have few options.

Please know that this is always your home. Now, it's your home like it is for René and Jill. We will always be glad to see you when you stop by. I will miss the spontaneous trips to the gym, the quick cup of coffee, or the spur-of-the-moment updates on what's going on in your life, but sooner or later, I would miss those anyway. I guess now's the time.

We love you Ben. I worry about some of the "habits" that you have but I also know that we've tried to give you the resources you need to do well. Use them wisely and you will come out fine.

Love,
Dad

So what does a father do when talking has no effect, when spoken words are like vapor and smoke that blow away unheard? I know what I did. I wrote. To this day I don't know if he ever read the letters I gave him. Some of them I'm not sure I ever delivered; like the days when I would talk to him— to myself—when he was not there. I may have written my feelings just to "get them off my chest" and then tucked the letters away in some obscure folder in my computer, forgetting them until a day when I find them while looking for something else. They are like scars, reminders of a wound.

I don't remember when I wrote this letter. I only know that it was not the last time we gave up and evicted him. In the coming months and years we will "evict" him over and over again.

14

I remember someone saying, "We've childproofed our home, but they get in anyway." I smiled, but it was a rueful smile because when Ben comes home it isn't through an open window or an unlocked door, it is through a crack in our heart. There will be the glimmer of hope that convinces us that this may be the time; this might be the moment when we the prodigal comes home.

I remember a camping trip when Ben was a young teen. It was just Ben and I—a dad and son weekend in the wilds of Oregon. We made our way into the mountains in search of some remote lake where we could lay out our sleeping bags, toss some mac 'n cheese into a pot along with some tuna and peas and cook up a manly portion of "tuna tetrazini."

The way to our first destination wasn't very well marked; moreover a survey crew had been through so that every direction looked like the trail. A check of our map and compass revealed that we were not where we should be so we made our way back to the car to look for another place to camp for the night.

I let him drive on the back roads.

After a night by the river we set out for another lake in the morning. That one we found.

In the afternoon we decided to hike to an abandoned lookout. As we hiked, Ben would charge off the trail and explore: rolling rocks down the slope, toppling dead trees, balancing on fallen logs. For the most part, I stayed on the trail watching, encouraging, cheering, but most of all making sure that he didn't wander too far, and that he could see where I was and find his way back to the trail.

I suppose that's why our home was never really childproof. On that campout I realized that one of my most important roles as a father was to remain on the trail so my son

15

would know how to get back. I wanted him to be able to count on it.

There is an old hymn that says,

Prone to wander, Lord I feel it
Prone to leave the God I love;
Here's my heart, O take and seal it,
Seal it for thy courts above.

How many times have I wondered off the trail? Many. Perhaps there will be many more, God forbid. But if he cannot forbid it, as I could not forbid Ben, I know this: my Father is there...as he always has been and always will be, waiting for this prodigal to come home.

(5) IDENTITY

And there were three men went down the road
As down the road went he:
The man they saw, the man he was,
And the man he wanted to be.

The letters started coming when Benjamin was about 18, official looking correspondence with his name on it and "Army National Guard" printed in the upper left corner of the envelope. They were the first indication of what our son intended to do. Ever the "man of mystery," he was embarking on an adventure without us, a search for identity.

There are some things a man has to do on his own. The truth was Ben had been making his own decisions for some time.

I knew that children eventually must assert their independence. Parenting is all about raising independent, capable people and then releasing them into the world to make their mark. A good father doesn't want to hold his son back; he wants his son to spread his wings and fly; to be a better man than he. A good father assures his son that he has what it takes to be a man. Toward that end, he tries to pour into his son the resources he will need to make the right choices when the day of decision arrives. But for Ben, when the days of decision came, the ones walking ten blocks to school or the ones at the recruiting office, his decisions came from some guarded place, inscrutable to everyone, maybe even himself.

Why?

The question remains unanswered to this day. Why are you doing this? Why did you do that? How could you not see…They are questions we stopped asking him, though in the quiet of our own guarded place they hang like ice-sickles, frozen in our thoughts.

I remember a conversation with him one night driving home from somewhere. He revealed that in his junior high years he had come to the conclusion that he had to be the rebel and the "wild child", it was the only role left to him. His older sisters, his only siblings, were models of success. René, the oldest was student body president, valedictorian, a picture of poise and competence. Jill was a dramatist, outgoing and friendly, liked by seemingly everyone. She was the choice of the student body to represent the school in the city's annual festival.

So, what was left to little brother? How could he compete with presidents and princesses?

In Genesis, Jacob passes himself off as his brother, Esau, to his blind father by wearing on his arms and neck the skin of a goat. Jacob pretended to be someone he was not in order to acquire the honor of the firstborn son. The honor rightly belonged to Esau but he was indifferent to his destiny. Significantly, Jacob thought himself worthy of the honor. It was not his intent to pass himself off as a goat.

Was that it? Did our son think the bar was too high and then decide not to risk the attempt in spite of our assurances? Rather than aspire to honor did he decide to just pass himself off as a goat? I don't know.

I do know that Ben set out to find something that he can't articulate and that I can't discern with certainty. The search motivated him to become a soldier. I suspect it was a search for identity in a place none of us, neither parents nor siblings, could go. Yet, even in uniform, the battle rages. The uniform, the success, the achievement, hasn't been enough. Seeking one's identity is not the same as finding one's destiny. They are very different. Identity can be ephemeral—a bandage that cannot bind a wound.

I remember going through my early twenties. I have often declared that of all the seasons of my life, those years were most difficult. I desperately feared being trapped in a cage of menial and meaningless work. I wanted to matter. I wanted to rise and fulfill some kind of destiny.

But I was content in one thing: I was a dad. I remember arguing to myself that it didn't matter what I did for a living because being a father was the most important. I was convinced that my investment in the lives of our children was more valuable than any other. Nothing else really mattered. It was who I was. I wanted nothing else.

As noble as it sounds, making parenthood my defining quality meant that my identity was in my children. I could only be what they were. I could only succeed when they found success. If they failed, their failure was mine. Fixing my identity in being a father meant that my children held the keys of destiny.

I suppose that is why Ben's flight into rebellion nearly toppled me. It cut at the root of who I thought myself to be. His efforts at becoming a man, misguided as they were, undercut the thing that made me a man.

Another lesson: if our identity is tied to people, even those we love, we can lose sight of who we are, and more importantly who God intends us to be. Paul reminded the church in Colossae that fulfillment in life was not in the earthly things it was hidden in Christ. He urged them to focus their attention on the things above. To do otherwise was to risk losing their destiny.

How often have I denied my destiny? How often has Ben? How many times has our search for identity persuaded us to eschew the honor of the son and pretend we are no more than a goat?

(6) REGRET

Be not like him who sits by his fireside and watches the fire go out, then blows vainly upon the dead ashes. Do not give up hope or yield to despair because of that which is past, for to bewail the irretrievable is the worst of human frailties.

~Kahlil Gibran

What is done is done and that which was not done must remain so. Therein is the dark soul of regret. Would that it were easy to just let go of it, set it adrift, put it behind me...forget. Alas, it is no simple matter to let go of regret. That which was undone remains, and that which was done is done, but regret means that it is never finished.

It's a useless emotion, really; still it is powerful because there is no remedy. It is the best case when the consequences of failure and miscalculation only impact us. It is mournful when our children must learn to live in spite of them.

But, what exactly is it that I regret? What, specifically, did I do or leave undone? Was I a drunkard? Was I unfaithful to my wife? A workaholic, never home? Was I cold and distant, absent and unapproachable? Perhaps, I was just dull and uninteresting, a half-man without admirable qualities. Maybe, I was too good; the bar was too high and unattainable. We should have gone camping more; had a family activity...we should have...

I can't put my finger on it. I see the condition of Ben's life and know I played a part in it. It was I who raised him so it must have been I that sowed the seed of despair and hopelessness. But when? How?

I used to be confident that I was doing right thing and that my parenting was impeccable—at least adequate. As the years pass, though, I become less and less certain that what I did was right. Nobody warned me that the curse of age might well be self-doubt, and the burden of time, perplexity.

Thinking back, I remember pulpit teachings and radio broadcasts; books and the family conferences. They all seemed to suggest that a parent needed only to observe some time-tested methodology and the result would surely be a godly family and problem-free kids. Go to church. Read the Bible. Pray—with and for your children; pray as a family; be firm; be clear; be consistent; dare to discipline, and all would be well. "Train up a child in the way he should go and when he is old he will not depart from it."

I believed all that, which is probably why I wasn't terrified of having children. Maybe that was a good thing. Had I known that children didn't do "by instinct" what was in all the books, I might have rejected the idea of having children at all. Had I known that sometimes kids make their own choices no matter how much a parent pours into them I may have been paralyzed with fear. Had I known how much nature rages against nurture…had I known that circumstances in the world can knock the props out from under a family, maybe I would have…

What? Would I have done anything different? Would I have declined parenthood and raised golden retrievers or chickens?

Unthinkable.

The fact is all that instruction wasn't wasted. There was truth in it. But life doesn't abide by a strict code of cause-and-effect. There's more to it than dropping in the correct change and receiving the desired product. There are extenuating circumstances, unexpected influences, and the "series of unfortunate events."

Yes, I have regrets. They are irritating and prickly like a speck of dust in my eye that won't wash out, or an invisible sliver in my skin that I can't see to remove. I wish I could go back and do more of whatever it was that was good, and less of whatever it was that was bad. But there it is: I would go back…because Ben is important to me. I would set things right if I could.

Even God had regrets. In the days of Noah He said, "I am sorry that I have made them." Then he gave instructions to Noah to build an ark so that all would not be lost when God cleansed the earth of the horror that had overtaken His prodigal race. The story of Noah is the story of a flood of divine despair, but it is also the story of unrelenting love. The human race was important to the Father as my children are important to me. The ark was God's refusal to give up. Centuries later He will say through the prophet Jeremiah the words that were undoubtedly in His heart as he agonized over the coming cataclysm, For I know the plans I have for you…They are plans for good and not for disaster, to give you a future and a hope.

And the ark was His willingness to go back, not because of what He had done wrong (He is God, after all) but because He had the heart of a father—The Father. Perhaps that is where regret comes from: intense and unquenchable dreams for the future of the ones we love. Perhaps that is why dads all over the world cannot give up and would gladly go back if they could. Perhaps when His heart was broken the Heavenly Father flung the pieces out upon humanity where they, like seeds, sprung up in the souls of men.

Thoreau said, "To regret deeply is to live afresh." It may be that I don't need to know what I did wrong. As I have often pointed out to others, including my children, "you can't start from where you were. You can only start from where you are." Regret looks back. Better that I should look forward. "Train up a child," the scripture says, "and when he is old he will not depart from it." As time passes, there may yet be a future and a hope.

(7) UNIQUENESS

I was in the basement when, my son-in-law, came down the stairs.

His voice was hard and his face was angry: "Where is Ben?" Robert is a police officer and he wasn't happy.

"Outside, in back," I answered. Almost before I was finished, he was headed back up the stairs.

I didn't know exactly what had happened, but it had something to do with what Ben had said to his sister, Jill, while he was drunk. He had tried to fix the blame for his life and circumstances on Jill--something about always having to measure up to her, having to measure up to both sisters. It had upset her and made her cry and Robert was furious. Jill was Ben's sister, but she was Robert's wife and suddenly this was between two men. Jill deserved an apology and Robert was determined she would get it.

It didn't come to blows, but it could have. I wouldn't have stopped it. Honestly, I didn't blame Robert. Not even a little.

The prodigal journey may seem like a lonely road traveled by a solitary wayward son, but it rarely is. There are those who love him who are invariably swept along in the wake of his wandering. Parents, of course, bear the agony of doubt and the despair of helplessness. But there are the brothers and sisters who also bear a burden—collateral damage. They are the ones to receive the blame and suffer the disappointments. They are the quietly turning wheels that need no grease.

It was my daughters that had caused me to anticipate the junior high and high school years with eagerness and optimism. I had watched each of them emerge from childhood with their own uniqueness and promise. So different from each other, yet complimentary in their character and personality! René, the organizer, leader and the articulate writer—student body president. Jill was the consummate dramatist and incurable romantic, friendly and compassionate. Later we watched in amazement as she became something of an adventurer.

And Ben! Enthusiastic and energetic; sharp as a tack and curious! We didn't know what would spark his interest, but we had no reason to doubt he, too, would find his unique place. We told him so.

We knew enough not to compare our children. We were always careful to treat them as individuals and assure them that they had their own place. But sometimes assurances aren't enough. Sometimes it is the voice of uncertainty that speaks the loudest and drowns out all others. It is that same voice that lashes out and damages those that love the most.

After awhile Jody and I made a conscious effort not to talk to the girls about their brother. It shouldn't always be about him. We should be able to focus on them. They were doing so well, he was acting so foolishly. They deserved the attention, not the prodigal who demanded it by behaving in ways that could not be ignored: getting the family car impounded; disappearing on Christmas Eve; getting drunk at family gatherings; being the subject of a frantic search on the morning of his sister's wedding in which he was to be an usher...

Eventually, we tried to steer the conversation away from Ben when we talked to our daughters. Their brother was not their problem; he was our problem. They had done the right things, after all. So, we tried to travel the prodigal journey alone, even though our daughters were the most likely to understand. But they had already given enough. Over the years they had given away the attention they may have needed while we tried to hold things together.

That's how the journey gets lonely as time goes on. There are fewer people you can talk to about "your son" because there is so much to say that sounds like what has been said before. It becomes tedious, tiresome and unfair.

I can understand the older brother in Jesus' story. He did right. His brother squandered his inheritance and exhausted the father with worry. So what did he get for his sacrifice? Eventually, the assurance of his father's love, I suppose. Love in the prodigal story has nothing to do with performance, it just is. Love is there. It covers the multitude of sins and acknowledges the abundance of virtue. It does both simultaneously. Love is the source of the pain that covers the sin; it is the foundation of the pleasure that acknowledges the virtue. In the midst of it all, love endures. The apostle, Paul, was right when he said that love hopes all things and endures all things.

There is no jealousy or bitterness that I can detect between Ben and his sisters. They love each other. The girls may not understand their brother but they love—even like—him. I think their peace comes from the knowledge that there is a unique place still waiting for Ben. Every valley brings him closer to it. They believe—as I want to—that he will come home one day. When he does, unlike the brother in Jesus' story, I think my two daughters will gladly join the party.

27

(8) GRACE

They sit in straight, green rows; military haircuts—high and tight; eyes forward in hardened stares; backs, rigid as fence slats, pressed to metal folding chairs; hands, palms down, immovable.

Six weeks ago they were just kids, now they are soldiers trained to defend the honor of their country. Trained to kill the enemies of freedom, and to be killed themselves if necessary. They will soon be deployed to Iraq. Some will not come home.

Ben sits across the aisle from us. He looks like a soldier. On his face is written the resolve of manhood. My mind wanders. I remember a towheaded first grader waving from the stage at the school assembly. I recall the fourth grader, an earnest shepherd in the church Christmas pageant. And I remember the uncertainty of junior high when we feared we were losing our grip and high school when the fear became reality.

Now, we sit in the assembly area at Fort Sill. We traveled across the country in order to be here, knowing this would be the closest thing to high school graduation that we would share with our son. We had to forego the customary recognition of achievement, the senior graduation party, and baccalaureate, the cap and the gown, and the stroll across the stage to shake the principal's hand and accept the diploma. We tell ourselves that succeeding in basic training is just as good—maybe better. Our son has accepted a challenge and risen to meet it, emerged victorious. I have to admit that I am proud. Not only that, I trust him. The defense of the nation is in capable hands. I can see it in the salute, in the parade outside after the ceremony. These are men.

I believe in them. I believe in Ben. I have faith in him.

A few days later we are waiting at the airport back home. He is flying in today. He will step off the plane in the uniform of proud manhood. He will embrace the discipline and rugged resolve that he learned from those weeks under the ruthless tutelage of his drill instructors who he started out hating and then learned to respect. He will carry all that into the monthly routine of the National Guard and into a new life of discipline and accomplishment.

But he is not on the plane. He calls and tells us that in the confusion one of the other guys accidentally made off with his ticket.

I believe him. I spend hours on the phone explaining the situation to the airline, trying to arrange for a refund of the 300.00 dollars he is spending for another ticket.

So why did I believe him? Because I wanted to. Perhaps I needed to. As it turns out, I was probably the only one who did. Months later, we learned that the night before he was to board the plane for home he had gone out drinking, came back to the motel drunk, and slept through his flight the next morning. Nobody else in the family seemed surprised, as though they had known that all along. I had put my faith in a soldier, forgetting that it takes more than a uniform to make a man.

Here's the thing: I still believe in him. Somehow, through the drunkenness and the partying, the cigarettes and the gambling, I can see the man. I love him for who he is, and I am convinced that he is not the hapless drunk or the careless reveler. I see what he will become tomorrow and that image shines brighter than what he does today.

Brennan Manning said, "God loves us as we are not as we should be. None of us is what we should be."

Maybe that's what the Bible means by grace. Maybe God's unfathomable ability to see through the stink and filth that I wear like fine robes is what is called grace. Above all the theology and biblical explanation, perhaps grace is nothing more than this: my Father believes in me. He believes enough that He is willing to lay down his life for me again and again so that one day I can shake off my foolish finery and emerge as a man.

It is written:

I am confident that the Father, who began the good work within you, will continue his work until it is finally finished on the day when Christ Jesus returns. [1]

---

1 Philippians 4:6 (PAR)

(9) LISTENING

I have been talking to him for an hour and for what? He isn't even here. He may be sleeping over at a friend's house, or hanging out in some bar. Wherever he is he's not here to receive the benefit of my "wisdom." I've been talking into the air, telling it how I feel. Explaining to furniture why what he is doing is going to lead him nowhere. Telling the steering wheel in my car how he should handle his money and how to break out of his toxic relationships.

Blah. Blah. Blah. Wind and vapor. All the words I've ever spoken in my solitary frustration, if written down, could fill a library.

Why do I do it? Maybe it's because if I don't I feel I will explode, or maybe if I tell an imaginary "him" how I feel, he will somehow feel it himself.

"Ben," I say, earnestly, "what if God has a destiny for you? You don't have to take it, but it's there with your name on it? What if there is a destiny and it's beautiful, more beautiful than you can imagine? Why not take a chance and reach for it…"

The words are dead leaves drifting in the air. Nothing changes. I sit in exhausted, foolish silence. He is not here, and even if he were, he would not hear. That, I conclude from experience. And perhaps that is why I speak into the air, because I can at least pretend that he hears, even though, for a dozen years, he has easily weathered my attempts to teach him, my words settling around him like dead leaves.

Such is the futile passion of the father of the prodigal. Listen! For God's sake, LISTEN!

From out of the silence comes a new lesson: If my passion—frustration—can drive me to speak to the air, what of my Father in heaven? Calvin Miller wrote,

> *It is strange how oftentimes the air speaks.*
> *We are sane as long as we hear voices*
> *when there are none.*
> *We are insane if we hear nothing,*
> *worse, we are deaf.*

Has Father been speaking? In his frustration with his prodigal son, have his words been falling around me like rain? And I not listening? Deaf.

I speak into the air while my Father speaks from it, calling the sinner, admonishing the unruly child. Only, unlike Ben, I am there; I am there because the Father is—He is always where I am.

The psalmist wrote:

Where can I go from Thy Spirit? Or where can I flee from Thy presence? If I ascend to heaven, Thou art there; if I make my bed in Sheol, behold, Thou art there. If I take the wings of the dawn, if I dwell in the remotest part of the sea, Even there Thy hand will lead me, and Thy right hand will lay hold of me. [1]

God does not speak to the air, He speaks to me. I know He wants to be heard by me because I know I want to be heard by my son. Father said,

"Take to heart all the words by which I am warning you today, that you may command them to your children, that they may be careful to do all the words of this law. For it is no

empty word for you, but your very life, and by this word you shall live long in the land..." [2]

Francis Schaeffer put it simply: God is there and He is not silent.

I am here, but am I listening?

---

1 Ps 139:7-12 (NAS)

2 Deuteronomy 32:47 (ESV)

(10) DEVOTION

Who takes the child by the hand takes the mother by the heart.

~German *Proverb*

Two other families—friends that grew closer even as our children were far away—had sons that went off to war with Ben. We fathers bore the terror of war alone. Though we never spoke of it, we understood one another. As men will do, the three of us let the truth of our private fear remain unspoken. We assumed it. For us, that was enough.

It was not enough for the mothers. The women would not leave their fears unspoken or their devotion unexpressed. They were the mothers, the ones who had known each of our three sons for the longest time. It was they who had felt the first sensation of life brushing against them deep inside. They had felt the turning in their womb; the sure knowledge that life was growing in the depths of themselves. These were the ones who knew the lives of their soldier sons most intimately. War had taken their children by the hand, and taken them by the heart.

No sooner than the boys had gotten their orders, Jody had determined that she, too, would go to war, and that she would not take up the weapons of the Spirit alone. There was a way in which real war, with uniforms, weapons and roadside bombs helped clarify the battle that she knew was being waged over Ben; and with clarity came determination.

She committed to get together with the others every Monday morning to pray. They were going into battle as surely as the children they had raised. They would encourage one another. They would hope together, pray together, and fear together. Unthinkably, they would one day grieve together.

The platoon of mothers still meets. The battle is different now, but it rages on. Wars have a way of coming home with those who fought them. Sometimes it comes home with an uneasy quiet, brooding. It comes home seething, restless and desperate. And sometimes it comes home cold and empty, its presence felt in endless absence. That is why Jody still meets with her "battle buddies" on Monday. The mothers fight on with fierce devotion.

Here, too, I see the heart of God, the compassion of my everlasting Father. His devotion to his children—even me—is unflagging. It is proclaimed in the travail of mothers who will not relent in prayer; who know instinctively that their voices are heard in the innermost shrines of heaven. It is written:

... a voice is heard, crying and weeping loudly. Rachel mourns for her children and refuses to be comforted, because they are [gone]. But I, the LORD, say to dry your tears. Someday your children will come home from the enemy's land. Then all you have done for them will be greatly rewarded. So don't lose hope. I, the LORD, have spoken. [I have heard the children] moan and say to me, "We were like wild bulls, but you, LORD, broke us, and we learned to obey. You are our God—please let us come home. When we were young, we strayed and sinned, but then we realized what we had done. We are ashamed and disgraced and want to return to you."

...you are my own dear children. Don't I love you best of all? ... I want you to be near me, so I will have mercy on you. I the Lord have spoken. [1]

As I watch the relentless prayer of these three mothers I take courage. Father hears such prayers. The praying may not appear to be bearing fruit, but there is hope. Their prayers are stored like seeds for a future harvest; or wait like a child unborn. Perhaps that is why these mothers have continued to pray together even after the sojourn in a distant land has ended. Perhaps it is because a mother knows how to wait. The apostle, Paul, wrote to the church, "My children — I am again undergoing birth pains until Christ is formed in you! I wish I could be with you now...." [2]

---

1 Jeremiah 31:15-20 (CEV with edits)

2 Galatians 4:19-20

(11) TRUST

Nearly three hours delay in my flight. Twice we push off from the gate, finally, the third time we are airborne. My cell phone is tucked in my bag, silent and useless. I am deaf to what is happening a world away in Iraq. Five soldiers were killed in a rocket attack last night at Taji.

Ben is stationed in Taji. It is a little less than 20 miles north of Baghdad.

Yet again I wait for news. There are thousands of soldiers at Taji. What are the chances? Small. But not zero. People win big money at the track on long odds. Five soldiers lost their lives in the gamble of war. Was Ben one of them? I didn't know—couldn't know. My cell phone is dead under the seat in front of me, in a bag. All the way to Minneapolis I think about it—silent, tucked away in a bag, dead.

Ben called last night. Did he call before or after the explosion that blew apart five families? We think the call came after the attack, that it may have been Ben's way of telling us he is OK, though he made no mention of rockets or fatalities. On the other hand, they are not supposed to leak information like that. The Army wants to be the first to bring the news to the families. If the attack came after Ben's call we may be one of them. Perhaps a U.S. government car with its somber passengers will be pulling up in front of our house while I am away. That's how such news comes to a family—this, we will learn from friends in the weeks to come.

I pray, affirm my confidence in the hand of God. Then I pray again as my confidence evaporates...and again. I got on to the plane with that uncertainty. As it lands in Minneapolis I am numb. When it reaches the gate I reach for my cell phone and resurrect it, fearing there may be a voicemail alert. I do not want to hear the electronic chord that signals a message is waiting. I stare at the display, fearing, waiting. I watch my name scroll across the screen. No voice mail alert. I start to tuck the phone back into its pouch I realize that I have not been breathing. And then...

Beep—beep—beep.

My heart pounds. There is a sick feeling in my stomach. I punch *86 and wait. "You have one unheard message. First message..."

Ben did not die that night at Taji. Sorrow touched some other family—five families. My daughter had called the paper and learned that the report of the attack had come across the wire before Ben called—she had left the news on my voicemail. Ben was alive.

And I learned how truly helpless I am. Whether sealed up in a metal tube at 36,000 feet with my cell phone off and my heart in limbo, or walking from the bedroom to the kitchen to pour my morning coffee, my life is out of control. The closest I come to it being in control is by knowing, by assembling information into a coherent picture that I only think I understand. I clamor for clarity, which is my best substitute for trusting God.

"Clarity," said Mother Teresa, "is the last thing you must give up. I have never had clarity. What I have is trust."

That is the lesson of the prodigal journey. Confidence and clarity are illusions, and my trust in God is feeble, that is why I have to constantly reaffirm it. Each time it crumbles under the weight of circumstance, I affirm it, hang on to what trust I have. Prayer is my *86:

You have one unheard message. First message:

Trust in the LORD with all your heart; do not depend on your own understanding. Seek his will in all you do, and he will show you which path to take. [1]

---

1 Proverbs 3:5-6 (NLT)

(12) FAITH

It was 2004. The year from hell.

We had received pictures over the Internet from David, the son of some family friends. He was a friend of Ben, too—a guardian in some respects. David was older and outranked him and had taken a special interest in him. He had covered for Ben on more than one occasion.

One of the pictures shows David lifting a smiling Iraqi child above his head. Another shows him and Ben surrounded by admiring children.

But my favorite is of Ben kneeling on top of a humvee next to an Iraqi child—eight or ten years old, maybe. The little boy has cut himself and Ben is bandaging his foot. There is the child and there is Ben, in full battle gear, gently pressing a bandage on the wound. Every time I looked at the picture—and I studied it often that year—I would notice Ben's hands. I would always notice his hands. Gentle. Capable. It was that picture that I showed any time someone asked if I'd heard from Ben.

I was proud of those photos. So many times I had felt shame concerning him—drunkenness, smoking, carousing—yet those pictures suggested a man of compassion and courage and tenderness. The kind of man, I told myself, that I had raised him to be. Every time I feared I was kidding myself I would imagine that the world of conflict, being thrown into the throat of hell, being faced with the cruel economics of kingdoms at war, was somehow bringing out the best in him. In those days I prayed that the wealth of spiritual strength in him would rise up in the field of battle and he would come home having left behind the foolish choices of his youth and return a man of character and integrity, hardened in courage and resolve, but tender and compassionate over the suffering he had seen.

English author and poet, Vera Brittain, wrote, *"The courage of greatness is adventurous and knows not withdrawing, but grasps the nettle danger with resolute hands, and ever again gathers security from the sting of pain."*

Surely, Ben would return from the war having gathered security from the sting of pain. Or so I persuaded myself. To face the headlines every morning and dread the reports of casualties, wondering if our son was among them, would have been too much without some hope that the war was working good in him and not exacting a penalty.

But war always exacts a penalty. When darkness closes in it drains the life out of us, whether in the devil's sandbox of Iraq, or the devil's playpen here at home. To imagine that Ben would come back healed was folly, just as much as it is foolish to expect that I can breech the border of sin here at home and not pay a price. The enemy may not take my life, but he surely batters my soul.

Perhaps that is what it is to come to faith. To meet the enemy on the field of battle and emerge with our lives, and then to suffer the terrors of memory that drive us to the healer of our soul. It is not war that heals us; it is surrender to the Prince of Peace. I think of the moment that Simon Peter declared his courage in the face of a battle that he knew nothing about. Jesus explained to him the cost of faith:

Simon, Simon, Satan has asked to sift each of you like wheat. But I have pleaded in prayer for you, Simon, that your faith should not fail. So when you have repented and turned to me again, strengthen your brothers. [1]

I had never noticed the real nature of Satan's demand. He had demanded to sift them all, not just Peter. It was Peter that Jesus had prayed for particularly. Why? So that in his recovery from the horror of the war, his faith would emerge tried and strong so that he could lift the others.

Ben did not come home healed. He came home sifted like wheat. The war in Iraq followed him home in nightmares and flashbacks—post-traumatic stress they call it. It followed him into every bar and party; pursued him and sifted him. It continues to this day.

But I still pray for him, even as Jesus prayed for Peter on the eve of his greatest fear and failure. I pray that Ben will one day turn and strengthen others. I pray that way because it seems to me that Jesus prayed for all of us—we all face the devil's threshing floor.

Whether Ben will return from the battle to strengthen others—or return at all—I cannot say. Not all soldiers go to the threshing floor and live. Indeed, David, the soldier that strengthened Ben, died in Iraq.

---

1 Luke 22:31-32 (NLT)

(13) GRIEF

I have a picture of the three of them. They are standing in our kitchen, arms around each other's shoulders, grinning. David and Jon are Ben's friends. They are our friends, too, as are their families. They are all gathered for a going away barbecue. Ben, Jon and David are going off to war.

The "two-of-the-one-six-two" was being deployed to Iraq and so we came together as families to see that our brave lads had a proper bon voyage. I remember that warm summer night. There was laughter and smiling; encouraging words; curiosity about "the mission," and burgers. I remember talking with Jim and George, the other two dads—kidding around. As I recall we hung out with the boys quite a lot that night.

I also remember thinking that we were frightened. We said nothing, of course, but inside the manly hugs, the teasing and the well-timed rejoinders we were scared for our sons. We had not raised these young men to be targets for fanatic adherents to a demonic religion; we had raised them to be the strong and handsome young men that they were. They were not to be objects of hatred in some faraway land. And so, brooding in the heart of each of us was fear, like an animal backed into a corner.

Soon, Ben, Jon and David—Shadrach, Meshach and Abednego—climbed onto a plane in Oregon, bound to climb off in the blazing furnace of war. And we three dads stepped into a nightmare of uncertainty, living day by day in the simmering shadow of doubt, of the terrifying question, "what if..." With every news report, the question seared itself into our consciousness. Another soldier ... two more marines ... helicopter down ... a roadside bomb.

What if...

In September Jody and I took off for Lake Tahoe. A friend had a cabin there and offered it to us for three or four days so we jumped at the chance to escape the usual. We arrived in the afternoon and unpacked; took a walk to shake out the kinks of the 12-hour drive; went out to eat; came back and sat on the deck; went to bed.

The following afternoon Jody called a few friends to let them know that a mutual acquaintance had been seriously ill and that prayer would be appreciated.

"Hi, Jim!" I heard Jody say into the phone. "Is Marylin...?"

A pause... "Hi, Mar..." Another pause...

And then the agony of war rushed in; an inferno of grief, as Jody gasped and then cried out—agony in a horrified wail that dissolved into brokenness and sobbing.

David was dead. Killed in action. A roadside bomb had stolen another firstborn son.

Suddenly, the innocence—there is no innocence in war—vanished. Any pretense that our children were immune from the "what-if" of war evaporated in the choking sob of a grieving mother: "Jody, he's gone! David is gone..."

And within the hour we were on the road. Plunging again into the reality of being a parent. It wasn't Ben that died on September 13, 2004, but it could have been. He had patrolled that same stretch of road just a day before. It was not Ben, it was one of our other sons, one of his friends, and we were headed home to be with his parents.

The sun hadn't yet appeared on the horizon; the Willamette Valley was still a misty grey. We were about an hour south of home. I had finally surrendered the wheel to Jody and was settling down to try to sleep a few minutes before we drove out to Jim and Marylin's. Then my cell phone rang...Hello?

"Dad? I need to ask you a favor."

It was Ben calling from Iraq. Somehow he had gotten hold of a satellite phone.

"Ben, we heard. We're on our way."

"I just wanted you to be with them."

"We're on our way. We're about an hour out. Are you all right?"

He said he was. But in the next few hours he would be taking care of David's personal effects, preparing them to be sent home.

For Jim, in the weeks after David's death, the question had changed. It was no longer, 'what-if?' it was, 'why me?' It ached in him every time he thought of David's smile and the reality that he would not see it again except in photographs and memory. But, eventually he began to ask, 'why not me?' Would he have preferred that another family, another father, endure the pain rather than he? Or isn't that the way this world is—this battlefield? The world is indifferent to suffering and loss. It is fathers who are not.

Does the eternal heart of God weep? We earthly fathers weep over our sons. Surely the heavenly Father weeps over his. When one of his sons is lost to him he must agonize. And what of it when a prodigal charges recklessly into the world— this furnace of war? Does Father fear for him? I know I fear for Ben because, unlike God, I do not know the outcome of this war. He may be home from Iraq, but the war is far from over. It rages in his heart and pursues him whenever he thinks of the day he retrieved David's things: ID tags, wallet, ring…the things he took from David's body the day he died, and the other things that were left back at the base, on that last morning. It was Ben who put all of them in a box and sent them home along with a letter to David's parents, the letter they read at their son's funeral.

(14) HONOR

We sat with Jim and Marilyn at a restaurant in the days of grief that followed the news of David's death. We talked about David and Jon, and Ben. We spoke of the war and of anger and grief. We reflected on loss and healing. And then they said they had something for us to hear: a letter that Ben had written.

~~

Posted: Taji, Iraq
Date: September 16, 2004

Dear Jim and Marilyn,

I am writing this letter to you shortly after returning from a trip to a FOB north of us where Lt. Perrin and I arranged for shipment of David's belongings. I have been waiting to write this letter until I could find the words that might closely reflect my emotions. This has yet to happen. I don't believe that there are words that convey the way we all feel. I want to express my sadness at the loss of David, and offer my condolences. As I cannot say this in person I hope that this letter will adequately convey my sentiments.

I need you both to know the pain this company is feeling, every man in this brotherhood feels the loss. David was an outstanding solider and set an example for many of the younger troops. His professional attitude and genuine caring for every person in his command made this loss incredibly difficult to bear. David and I didn't always agree, but without fail, it always became apparent that his convictions were in my best interest. He looked out for me, and all of us in a way that was selfless and diligent. I have many memories of him asking all of us what we needed, what we would like, if there was anything he could do for us. I've watched in amazement as he, on his day off (few and far between) would leave his room in the morning and go to take care of issues for us, not to return until well after dark. David would always return with news of his successes and usually a bag full of things we desperately needed. He would never take no for an answer, he never gave up and every time, he would return, like Santa Claus with presents for his boys.

I have been having a hard time accepting his loss; I have no way of ever imagining the pain you must be feeling. I think that our first sergeant said the words that most accurately described our feelings, with misty eyes he said to me "we've been robbed, they robbed us today".

I have many times listened to Dave talk about his experiences in the military, his accomplishments, his memories, and each time he would share these stories with us there was an overwhelming pride he conveyed. I used to come into our room in Fort Hood after David had fallen asleep and hear The Ballad of the Green Beret playing from beneath his headphones, and smile. His love of cadences and songs about the army remind me of the one thing that we can take comfort in, David loved his family, his country and his fellow soldiers. It was in defense of these things that he gave his life; it was in defense of those who could not defend themselves that he died. I know of a certain man who lived 2000 years ago who died for these same things.

David will be missed by all that knew him, but his memory will live on through all of us. When we hear the word 'patriot' we will remember. When we here the national anthem we will remember. When we salute our flag we will remember. Our country and the countless other countries David has defended will be our reminder of what it is to be an American, and more importantly what it is to be human. His example in life will not be forgotten in death, his name will be remembered among those who gave their all, so that others might live.

I am proud and honored to have known David, I will miss him, but I will see him again, in another army, in a better place, in the company of all who have fought for what is right. Until then David will be doing what he has always done: he will be watching us, protecting us, and waiting for us.

Love,
Spc. Benjamin Mayhew

~~

We wept together—two families touched by war. We wept at the loss and we wept at the glimpse of Ben's heart. David had shown special concern for Ben and that love had not gone unnoticed. Love is like a seed planted by a gardener. Sometimes it sprouts, healing as it grows. But the prodigal heart may be choked with weeds or filled with stones. The Gardener stands ready to cultivate it, but waits for the prodigal to yield. Meanwhile, those who watch from afar live in fear, knowing not every wanderer makes it home.

(15) SHAME

I had to admit it. I was ashamed. I dreaded the question that seemed so appropriate while he was away in Iraq: Have you heard from your son? Why, yes. We heard from him a couple of days ago. He says the temperature's been over a hundred and ten. They've been doing patrols. He's responsible for communications for his unit. We sent him about 60 pounds of coffee and some school supplies. The guys have been helping out a school there that has nothing for the kids. Thanks for asking. Keep him in prayer."

But after he returned, the answer required an admission that Ben was not doing well. Not that he wasn't doing exactly what he wanted—he was doing that. It was just I couldn't be proud of what he was doing.

"How is your son?"

"Oh, fine. He's been drinking a lot. He came home drunk last night. He passed out while he was climbing through the window. I had to pull him into the house and carry him to bed. And did I mention that he's unemployed and collection agencies keep calling? Thanks for asking. Now, if you will excuse me I have to decide whether to slam my fist into a wall or try to find a lonely place to cry."

The war came home with our son. Sometimes it feels as though we are fighting the insurgency in our own basement. Would that we could blame it all on the war, but the truth is much of the behavior that is so painful now was happening long before he deployed to the Middle East. War only made it worse.

We know, of course that a family should never try to travel the prodigal journey alone. We know that we should share our suffering with reliable friends who will hold us and pray for us, and for Ben. And so we have. And they have. That is good…but it is also painful, because sharing the pain of the journey means that they will ask the obligatory question: How is your son doing?

Failure and shame: the admission that he is not doing what we wish he were. Evidently, we have not raised our child well. For me it is the admission that I have failed as a father; failed to impart godly values; failed to nurture the relationship, common bond and friendship that every father wants with his son. I had one chance in life to raise a son and could not do it. I look back and try to figure what I did wrong and it always comes up the same. Failed…failed…failed, and you don't even know why.

Shame is the painful feeling arising from the consciousness of something dishonorable, improper or ridiculous done by oneself or another. How often have I brought shame on my heavenly Father? Have I always been the son that Father would be proud of, and worthy of His name? Have I not been stubborn? Devious? Profane? Self-indulgent?

Undoubtedly. Without question.

Father doesn't make excuses for my behavior, nor does He blame Himself for my weaknesses. More often, I would guess, he grieves over the wounds that I use as excuses for selfishness and rebellion. In the end, it is not He that is responsible for my choices; it is I. God did not feel shame over the rebellion of His people. Instead, He lamented:

"But My people did not listen to My voice, And Israel did not obey Me. So I gave them over to the stubbornness of their heart, To walk in their own devices. Oh that My people would listen to Me. [1]

The Father still knows that desire to call out to his children—to call out to me. I know He knows because I, too, have that desire. He had it first.

Yes, I have shamed my Father. My son has shamed me. We have shamed ourselves in the process. But God is not ashamed of me, nor is He ashamed of Benjamin. I shouldn't be either. To be ashamed makes it about me. All about me—what others might say about me when I'm not around. What they might think...of me. And I realize that to be ashamed of Ben is a selfish thing. Moreover, it isn't how God thinks, so it shouldn't be how I think.

It is not I that is responsible for my son's choices; it is he. That others are willing to blame me for them (though, I suspect that most don't) is really not my concern. If I make it my concern it is evidence that I have taken Ben's wounds and made them secondary to my reputation.

Rather, my Father in heaven bids me stand with Him—unashamed—and join his lamentation: How often I wanted to gather you in my arms and protect you. How often I wanted to help and heal. How often...

---

1 Psalm 81:11-13a (NAS)

(16) YEARNING

He got into an accident last night in a borrowed car. Mark, the car's owner, called us to tell us. The car was impounded and Ben was nowhere to be found. Apparently, he had given Mark's name at the scene of the accident and then fled.

Mark was an officer in Ben's guard unit. More than that, though, he was a friend. I'd heard Mark say that Ben was probably as close to a son as he was likely to have. On the basis of that friendship, he had loaned Ben his Jeep. When the call came from the police, he was deeply hurt. How could such kindness be returned with such selfishness and disrespect? Mark was heartbroken, betrayed.

I know those feelings. I thought as a parent they were uniquely mine. It never occurred to me that prodigals inflict the same hurts on others as well. Hurts are the careless legacy of the prodigal—scraps left along the trail of the wanderer.

Yet, if I feel betrayed and hurt, the Father of heaven must also feel those things. The wayward trail of the wanderer crisscrosses the heart of God, too—I see my own boot prints there.

I pause at the gate of the garden where I come to pray, a monastery near my house, the hermitage of a sympathetic priest who graciously allows me to wander the grounds. It is early morning, not yet dawn. But the birds know it is coming. They seem to detect daybreak by premonition. Even when there is no sign of light, they begin the morning chorus. I envy that premonition, a sense that the night is over and the morning is near.

I wander the path, as much by memory as by sight. I find my favorite bench.

And I sit a long time in the dark. I imagine a joyous thing, a figure at a distance in the pre-dawn grayness. He walks slowly on the path, coming toward me, hands dug deeply in his pockets…

"Ben?

"Hi, Pops…" His voice is low and discouraged.

"What are you doing here?"

"I figured you'd be here."

I grab my towel, the one I bring to wipe the dew from the bench. I make a dry place for him to sit down.

"Do you want to talk?" I ask. I stare down into the coffee I bought on my way to the garden. "I would've brought coffee for you, but I didn't know you were coming." I pause, "it's bad coffee anyway…"

And then, he sits and we talk. What was it like in Iraq? How did you feel? What happened there? Were you scared? What happened last night? Are you OK?

It was a made-up moment. The place where I had wiped the dew from the bench was cold and empty. Didn't happen. It was just what I wished would happen. No judgment. No condemnation. No correcting or badgering. I just wanted to hear and get a glimpse of his heart.

I always wanted to be the kind of dad that he would want to talk to and confide in. I had that kind of dad. I guess that was my good fortune. I wish it had been Ben's.

I remember coming to pray here on another day. It had been a long while since I had come. I remember a strange impression—my heavenly Father was lonely. Does God yearn for my company? Does He feel the emptiness on those days when I have found other things to do rather than seek him out in the garden? While I labor in futility, burrowing deeper into sin; does he ache over my absence?

I remember another garden at another time. God came looking for his prodigal son who was hiding from his Creator...

"Adam, where are you?"

I sit alone as the darkness turns to dawn, having learned another lesson on this prodigal journey: Father yearns for me.

(17) GENERATIONS

I did some crying this morning.

There is a place in the garden where there is a pillar, a wooden obelisk standing in the center of a circular walk. On it is carved "Let there be peace on Earth," in four languages. It stands reaching into the predawn sky, a dark finger pointing to heaven. Here is where I pray for Ben. Nearly every morning while he was in Iraq I stopped here at the "Peace Pole" to pray. I still do as I pray for peace in his soul and for an end to war.

He is broke, unemployed, and homeless. I have determined that he must not live with us...again. He is 24 and ought to be taking care of himself. Nevertheless, he has been on our couch for the last two nights.

I stand at the pole praying. Suddenly, I imagine him standing there with me. I imagine introducing him to the Father. "Here is the one I've been talking about, Lord. Here he is..." And I break down. I drop to one knee and sob.

Introspection follows. I keep going back to the night when, as a child, he took scissors and cut up his favorite teddy bear. What did I think was going on there? How could I have not seen how deeply he was hurting and this was the only way he knew how to voice it?

There had been several deaths in the family. To Ben it must have seemed that childhood was no longer a safe place for him. And I did nothing to change that. Instead of pulling close, I assured myself that it was drama, just theater. I protected my emotions. I learned to do it as a child in my mother's world. I learned how to protect myself by seeing through the exaggerated emotional outbursts, the manipulation.

I began to look—to feel—as I would at a movie, reassuring myself that it was all a script and that the actors went home after the shoot and lived happily ever after. When she would attempt to rule my emotions I would filter them as I would at a movie. How often have I filtered my experience that way?

Before my nephew died I remember thinking his illness was not as serious as it really was—he'd be all right. I saw it like a drama. I know now that was a defense. I protected my emotions.

And I did the same thing that night as Ben raged against a childhood that no longer felt safe. Rather than hear and feel and enclose him and reassure him, I reassured myself. Only theatrics. Don't overreact. Steady, now. Don't freak out…So I was steady, unperturbed, and as I defended my emotions by letting that filter kick in, Ben began to flee from his own emotions.

It is said that our greatest strengths are our greatest weaknesses. I am known for being composed and unflappable, optimistic and positive about things. But the downside is I don't see how serious things are. When I strip the circumstances of their drama as I learned to do as a child, I sometimes tear away the true meaning. In this way, I may have failed my son and invited a dozen years of pain.

As I remember that night, the teddy bear, and the fireplace that was its destruction, it occurs to me that there were two children there. There was Ben, trying desperately to put a safe distance between himself and his emotions; and me, still the child trying to protect mine.

But over it all—in it—was the Father, the Creator-God that yearns over his fallen child-race and mourns with it. The Father said,

When Israel was a child, I loved him... But the more I called to him, the farther he moved from me...I myself taught Israel how to walk, leading him along by the hand. But he doesn't know or even care that it was I who took care of him. I led Israel along with my ropes of kindness and love. I lifted the yoke from his neck, and I myself stooped to feed him. [1]

The Father was determined to share the woundedness of His children and confront their rebellion. It would eventually lead Him to the cross. His love became crucifixion.

I remember the feeling of helplessness as Ben went off to war. I wished that I could take his place in order to keep him safe. Alas, I could not. Perhaps it is such a feeling that caused the Father to plunge into time and space. He soaked the war into himself, absorbing the hatred, accepting the pain, and healing the broken-hearted, though they did not know it.

In the end we, my son and I, are children left on the field of war, each wounded and frightened in our own way. His wounds bleed rebellion and ache in his addictions. Mine fester in regret. But here is the lesson and the hope: the Father's love is from generation to generation. The Psalmist wrote:

Just as a father has compassion on his children, so the LORD has compassion on those who fear Him. For He Himself knows our frame; He is mindful that we are but dust. As for man, his days are like grass; as a flower of the field, so he flourishes...But the loving-kindness of the LORD is from everlasting to everlasting on those who fear Him, and His righteousness to the sons of sons... [2]

---

1 Hosea 11:2-4 (NLT)

2 Psalm 103:13-17 (NAS)

(18) WRATH

I could read it in Jody's face. She was near tears; that middle ground between anger and deep hurt. It had happened again.

"Look in the basement," she said.

We made our way down the stairs, through the kitchen and then down another endless flight of stairs to the basement. From under the couch where Ben was sleeping, wetness, like a shadow, was clearly visible on the carpet.

"Ben!"

Nothing. He was sleeping.

I shook him, hard. "Ben! Get up!"

He stirred slightly. I grabbed his arm and pulled him upright. "Ben, you wet your pants all over the basement!"

Then came the usual harangue. What are you doing? What are you thinking? How could you? Would you...should you...will you...won't you...are you...aren't you...? He sat on the couch looking at the floor, maybe hearing, maybe sleeping, or maybe just indifferent.

My sister, opened the door of her basement bedroom and peered out to see what the commotion was.

I don't know what Jody was saying. Whatever it was, he stopped looking at the floor. I saw his face. Drunk. Stupid drunk. And then it happened...

He snickered; looked up and smiled.

Something snapped in me. A wild ferocity welled up. My hand shot out and grabbed his shirt. I pulled him from the couch and on to the floor—a clumsy, furious motion that threw me off balance. I stumbled backward against the wall, which caved against my weight. Then I was up and on top of him, arm coiled, hand clenched.

"DON'T YOU EVER LAUGH AT US! NEVER!" I was screaming. The fist tightened; my arm pulled back—a hammer raised. I tried to decide where the blow would fall, where to pour out the wrath, the fury, the righteous indignation.

"Dan!" It was my sister. "Don't! Don't. Stop!"

I stopped. I looked down at the face of my son. Where should I hit him? Jaw? Eye? Nose? Should I knock out the teeth that wore the braces that we had put on so that he would have an attractive smile? Should I open another gash in his forehead that would leave a scar, not from an accident on the playground, but from the wrath of his father? A scar that would fill my heart with regret every time I saw it?

The wrath drained away, fading to anger, like a festering boil in my soul. Yet there was something else in my soul: relief.

"Get out!" I told him. "Get out of my house. I don't want to see you here." And I shoved him toward the steps and pushed him up to the kitchen and out onto the deck.

"Nice yard, Stud," he said, and then sauntered over to the railing and leaned on it, facing away from me. I went back in the house and closed the door.

Jody was downstairs trying to dry out the carpet and peel the cover off the cushions on the couch so they could be washed…again.

Wrath. I haven't felt it often. Almost never. It leaves me weak and drained. Almost as though I wasn't built for it—too much to bear.

Have I ever slept through conviction, ignoring the reality of my sin, hearing what I want to hear, disregarding everything else? Or have I looked up at Father and smiled in my rebellion? Have I sauntered through life trying to keep hold of something like control, not wanting to admit that I have been foolish and that I have no power, that I am helpless?

These foolish, useless gestures! How much of my life have I spent posing? Trying to appear that I am doing exactly what I want to do, and should do, while all the time I have this gnawing sense that my life is spiraling out of control; that I am weak and needy. Haven't I persisted in rebellion, and worse, known instinctively that I deserved God's wrath?

Does my heavenly Father ever feel it? He must. The Bible talks about the wrath of God. There are some who think that wrath is what the Father is all about.

But is it?

Maybe wrath drains him, too. Maybe it is love that makes wrath a last resort. Perhaps my heavenly Father wants more than anything to see his son—to see me—with my face turned upward, not expecting the blows, even though I might deserve them, but smiling like a child when daddy comes home at the end of the day.

(19) TERROR

Somewhere in the conscious world, the world beyond sleep, the phone is ringing. I force my eyes open and glance at the clock on the dresser: it is well after midnight.

I grope for the phone. "Hello?"

"Dad?"

"Ben! What's up?" I try to sound awake, alert.

"He's dead. I killed somebody. It finally happened..."

I am sitting up now, fully roused. My heart is racing. My mind is a kaleidoscope of images: handcuffs, courtroom, mug shot on page three of the Metro section of the paper, prison all in a muddled instant. How many years for manslaughter, for murder?

"Ben, what happened?"

"He's not moving! I killed him. He's dead."

"Ben, where are you?" I can hear the desperation, the terror, in my own voice.

"Doesn't matter..." The desperation in Ben's voice has turned grey and heavy, like lead.

"Ben, where are you? What happened?" I can hear voices in the background and music, but no answer. "Ben?"

"Doesn't matter..."

The phone goes silent. He has hung up.

I fumble for the light on my dresser so I can read the caller ID on the phone. He has called from his cell phone. He could be anywhere.

Suddenly I am being drawn downward into a spiraling well of frantic despair. Jody is out of the country and won't be home until tomorrow. "How's Benjamin?" she will ask. What do I say to her? How do I tell her that our son called in the middle of the night to tell me that he has taken someone's life? That he is in jail charged with manslaughter or worse.

I stumble down the stairs to the living room, praying as I go. I go out on the front porch. If he called from somewhere nearby I should be able to hear sirens.

Silence. Only the din of cars in the distance. The air is the smell of midnight.

I sit on the top step of the porch praying into the damp darkness: "Father God, what do I do?" The phone is still in my hand. I call his number. Maybe he'll pick up.

He does.

"Ben, what happened?" There is music in the background. Laughter. Sounds of a nightspot.

"Doesn't matter…"

"Ben, where are you? I'll come and get you. We can figure this out."

"Too late. Doesn't matter." Again the phone goes silent.

What do you do when a thing is done that cannot be undone? Surely that is a taste of hell: floating without hope in a black nothing, no place to rest, no destination or relief from the emptiness, only the awful certainty that it is over, too late, doesn't matter. The unpardonable sin, some call it. The horrible imagining that at the end of a lifetime of chances, a person comes to the last one and loses it. Then is the moment of terror, followed by brooding hopelessness.

Occasionally, I have gone there in my own heart, wondered for brief seconds if I have walked off the precipice of existence into the void, the eternal consciousness of eternal life without hope of redemption.

Then I remember. Father is not willing for anyone to perish, but that all should come. Somewhere in the middle of the terror I stumble on the assurance that if I still care, that if it matters to me, then I am not dead, my spirit is yearning for its creator, for the Father and son reunion. As long as I breathe there is hope. There is more grace in God than sin in me. "Where are you?" asks Father God. "I'll come get you. We can figure this out."

Morning came after a sleepless night, and then a day. There were no reports of suspicious deaths in our city. No killers were sought, or "persons of interest."

Ben did not kill anyone that night.

I don't know exactly what happened—maybe a fight and a knockout punch and nothing more. Maybe a flashback to a death in battle half a world away. Anyway, he never told me. Perhaps he couldn't remember. Alcohol does that sometimes. Maybe that's a mercy.

But I remember two days of terror. I remember driving home from the airport the next day with Jody, dreading the question I knew she would ask. I remember having to tell her. We shared the terror. The reassurance didn't come all at once—no sudden sigh of relief. The nightmare merely faded, lost its potency, and it became clear that it never happened. And so, as new mornings came one by one, we dared again to breathe.

.

(20) SEEKING

The storm clouds are dark and threatening. Something has happened—we don't know what—and the downward spiral has begun.

"How's it going?" we ask our son, not wanting to seem nosey—the experts caution against that. But we recognize the signs of depression.

"Fine," he says, not looking away from a televised poker tournament.

"You seem down. Is everything OK?"

"Yeah, everything's fine..."

We know everything is not fine. We know that he is plunging into a black trench of discouragement. We know that something has triggered this. We also know from years of experience that it is pointless—futile—to ask or guess what the trigger was. The doors are closed. Solemn warnings or compassionate offers of solace will change nothing. Nothing we do or say will close the yawning pit in his soul. We let it alone. We have no other choice.

He rouses himself from the couch in front of the TV and leaves, walks out the front door, and lights a cigarette. Hands dug into his pockets, he strolls up the street.

Two blocks away is the Parkway Pub.

Another day out of a hundred days very much like it. Alcohol, the god of forgetfulness, beckons and we sit waiting.

Another day of worry. For me it will mean another night sleeping on the couch—"defending the furniture" we call it. If he comes home and sprawls on the sofa, he will fall asleep and wet himself before morning. We will awaken and have to strip the upholstery from the sofa and wash it; dry the cushions as best we can; scrub the carpet. So I sleep on the couch. If he comes home I will lead him to the army cot set up next to the furnace. There is plastic spread on the floor beneath it.

The only other option is preemptive. Go after him. Try to intervene before it's too late. I know some of the places. I, who hate cigarettes, drinking and gambling—I've watched the wreckage pile up in life after life—I push through the door of one tavern after another, sucked into the dark staleness of beer and smoke. Liquor bottles lining the shelves around the bar. Shadow-ghosts hunched over glowing video-poker terminals as soulless, disjointed tones promise quick wealth and more drinks.

I scan the darkness. Sometimes I get lucky: "Come on. Let's go home." Most times I'm not and I go home alone and sleep on the couch.

Jesus told a story:

What man among you, if he has a hundred sheep and has lost one of them, does not leave the ninety-nine in the open pasture and go after the one which is lost until he finds it? When he has found it, he lays it on his shoulders, rejoicing. And when he comes home, he calls together his friends and his neighbors, saying to them, 'Rejoice with me, for I have found my sheep which was lost!' I tell you that in the same way, there will be more joy in heaven over one sinner who repents than over ninety-nine righteous persons who need no repentance. [1]

I have thought about Jesus' story a lot over the years. It was about someone who had lost what he valued. The shepherd was looking for something important to him. Moreover, he was looking for that which was his and was vulnerable. To lose a sheep was to know that it wouldn't be long before, if it were found at all, it would be found dead, consumed by a beast of prey, its remains scattered on the ground.

Jesus' story was about the Father and about himself looking for the lost, looking for me.

Were there dark crags so foreboding that Jesus would turn back and give me up? Was there a damp ravine or rank pool that would have so repelled him that he would have counted me forever lost, the remains of my hopeless soul to be scattered like dry bones?

I have been found. I know the answer to those questions is 'no.' Corrie ten Boom wrote, "there is no pit so deep that God's love is not deeper still."

So, I remember those murky caverns; blue smoke hovering like a banshee over the pool table, the staccato wailing of the gambling machines and the empty faces staring at the TV screen that leers back, unblinking, from the corner above the bar. I remember and I know that it was never about defending the furniture.

---

1 Luke 15:4-7 (NAS)

(21) ENDURANCE

"New message left today at 4:02 AM..."

Oh, God. What now? We were away for three short days, a quickie vacation between commitments, courtesy of some friends who had a vacation home at Black Butte. Jody had foolishly decided to call home and get our messages. We should know better. Vacations, holidays, and retreats are an invitation to disaster. We don't know why. Maybe there is a spiritual thing that happens at such times that harass our son and, by extension, us.

The voicemail was Ben. Who else would call home at four in the morning? His speech is slurred. His voice sounds heavy and dark. "Hi ... I'm having a bad night ... I ... (unintelligible) ... all be over in 48 hours ... (unintelligible)... maybe ... I'll ... it will... (unintelligible) ..." And the message ended. Not enough information to tell what was going on, just the familiar, disoriented voice of alcohol and depression.

We called Kristi, his girlfriend. She said he had been home when she left for work so we breathed easier. We breathed easier again when a text message came at 1:23. It said: I love u mom and dad...

We resumed resting. And then came the call from his Kristi: "Are you still with Ben?" No, we weren't with Ben. We were in Central Oregon 120 miles from there. We hadn't seen him since we stopped by on our way out of town yesterday.

He had lied to her and said he was going to have lunch with us and now neither she nor we knew where he was. Call us if you hear anything, we say, and then quietly try not to notice the fear in one another's eyes.

I love u mom and dad...

The message that had encouraged us a few hours before was now filled with portent, as was the garbled voicemail. We were pulled into another waking nightmare. Forget about rest. Forget about play. Forget about a quiet dinner out. Remember the times when he cut himself. Remember that he has wondered aloud if life was worth it. Remember that on the night he wrecked his friend's car he sat alone with a gun, thinking...

We go bed and try to sleep. At midnight there is a new text message. It is from Kristi: We checked all the downtown bars and the area. No luck. We talked to our friends at the downtown police station and they will call if they hear anything...And so continues a night of dread. Was the lifetime he spent in Iraq any more fearsome than this eternity of dread?

"Father, please protect him. Please bring him home. Father, please..." I pray as I have a hundred times before. Then I imagine "the call"; the terrifying details; the personal effects; the funeral arrangements, and months—years—of mourning. Then I pray again, "Father..."

We awaken Friday. Neither of us got much sleep. We decide to pack up and go home. Why stay? To go for a long bike ride in the crisp autumn air? To make plans together? Soak in the hot tub? Maybe go for a walk? To wait for the phone call that we've feared for the last three years? To keep insisting in our minds that it will be OK this time, just like all the other times? To resist the irresistible fear that this time it may not be?

No. Let's go home.

We are stopped at the resort office to check out when the call comes from Kristi. He is home and in bed sleeping it off. Too late, now, to change plans. We head home ourselves, thankful and helpless; relieved and tired.

We are so tired.

I remember what Father-God told his son, Paul: "My grace is sufficient for you, because power is perfected in weakness." Perhaps that is what is to be gained as the fears gnaw away at my heart like rats. When fears overwhelm me, perhaps I am to learn to drive them away with shouts of, "Grace! Grace!" Perhaps there is where the power is. Even if the worst should come there is grace to endure.

Or if the great storm is over one day, not with a cry for mercy but a shout of triumph, if there should come the dawn of redemption and reconciliation, there will be grace for that, too. If that day should come—the answer to long labors of prayer—it will not be because of my great faith, confident strength, or courageous power, it will be by grace.

'Not by might nor by power, but by My Spirit,' says the LORD of hosts. What are you, O great mountain? ...you will become a plain; and he will bring forth the top stone with shouts of "Grace, grace!" [1]

---

1 Zech 4:6-7 (NAS)

(22) HOPE

"Ben seems to be fighting the last battle of faith. He is warring desperately, looking for a reason not to believe. I believe he is losing that war—thank God."

It was an entry in my journal dated over five years ago. It was a false hope. The battle rages on.

My journals have a number of such optimistic entries. They describe, however briefly, moments when the road seemed a little less bleak and unpredictable. I suppose anyone who travels the prodigal journey has those moments, like signposts bearing a single word: hope.

Hope is the fragrance of a day without the smell of alcohol, or a day when he is busy at work. Hope is the seed that is planted when he talks of the future, or when he has received accolades from others. Hope is the green leaf of spring when he chooses to spend time with a non-drinking friend; when he spends the day with his sister. Hope is the summer shower as he checks himself into rehab and as he returns with clear eyes and a purposeful look.

Hope is what makes enablers out of parents.

Hope makes us desperate to nourish whatever tender, green shoot appears in the crusted ground of the prodigal soul. It explains the hundred dollars—or thousand—to "get him on his feet." Hope breaks the hard-metal resolve to never let him move back home. When we see the faint evidence of responsible behavior appearing on the far side of yet another valley of desperate remorse we fling the door open and bid him come. Hope is the quality that pushes patience beyond the limits of human endurance. It incites the reckless attempt to rescue and the unexplainable willingness to forgive. Hope is all of that…until it finally decays into a habit. Hopes are raised and dashed, and disappointment builds upon disappointment until each new hope is like a butterfly tied to a stone. In an instant we dare to hope, but the weight of it is a burden.

The Bible says that hope doesn't disappoint. But it does. It disappoints every time it is fixed in the wrong place. The apostle Paul wrote,

…We rejoice in the hope of the glory of God. Not only so, but we also rejoice in our sufferings, because we know that suffering produces perseverance; perseverance, character; and character, hope. And hope does not disappoint us because God has poured out his love into our hearts by the Holy Spirit, whom he has given us.[1]

Real hope is an eternal thing; it is fixed in its place like a star and held there by the hand of the Father. That's the hope that does not disappoint. Lesser hopes, bound to lesser things, are not hopes at all, but wishes…dreams. The hope that does not disappoint is the flame that feeds the fire; it is kindled by faith and fueled by love. The hope that does not disappoint is why those who journey with the prodigal continue on. Dreams may fade and wishes not come true, but hope dies last.

Every seed we lay to rest
Every promise that's foretold
Every prayer we offer up on high
Every ship we point to harbor
Every hand we reach to hold
Every lonely voice that dares to question why
Every child we bring to birth

Every vision we unfold
Every dream that keeps us reaching for the sky

It is the cool breeze in the mineshaft
The shipwrecked sailor's dream
The message in a bottle:
We are more than we seem

Hope dies last
It is the flame that feeds the fire
Hope dies last
It is the dream that drives us higher
We revive and we remember
Not the first and not the last
Ever holding fast
Hope dies last. [2]

---

1 Romans 5:2-5 (NIV)

2 Hope Dies Last. Words & music by John McCutcheon - http://folkmusic.com. Appalsongs (ASCAP) 2005

(23) PROMISE

There is a photograph hanging in the upstairs hallway. Occasionally, I stop and look at. Sometimes for a minute or more I stand and ponder, gazing intently at the face there. It is my face—younger by 25 years, moustache, longer hair, barely into my thirties.

I was staring at it today and suddenly realized as I stood there in the hall that my expression was mirroring the younger me in the picture. Wonder. Just short of amazement.

In the photo I'm leaning over a clear plastic bassinette at the hospital gazing down at a tiny baby lying there. Somebody—I don't remember who—snapped the picture through the nursery window and captured that moment of wonder. A son! My son. I have two beautiful daughters and now a son. I wasn't sure I'd ever have a son. Not that I didn't want one—I think every man wants a son—we just weren't sure if it was wise, after two C-sections, for Jody to be pregnant again. We had been undecided and then the decision was made for us. We counted it a gift from God. I remember having that feeling with all three of our children.

The picture on the wall captured it. There in that bassinette was a living question mark; an empty canvas; a world of promise; dreams yet undreamed; hopes waiting to be fulfilled. There was my own flesh and blood waiting for my contribution to his destiny. I don't remember doubting for a moment that I would give him what was necessary to discover his place in the world. I didn't have any specific dreams for him—a family business to pass on, like my grandfather did to my father; or expectations that he would be a doctor, or a minister. I just knew he had a future and a hope.

As he grew and began to walk we would play children's songs for him: I am a promise. I am a possibility. I am a promise, with a capital 'P'!

I never doubted it.

But I never imagined that I would have to fight so hard against doubt. Sometimes it feels like life and death, this struggle.

My baby boy is in jail today. Not for life or anything. Not for years, or even months. Eight days is all. A little over a week for something he did while he was drunk. He narrowly missed being charged with a felony, but the brother of a close friend is an attorney—thank God for friends who have brothers who are ex-Marines that became attorneys! He argued for a misdemeanor and won it from a judge with a soft spot for veterans. And now, Ben is down at the justice center "doing time."

I asked him if he wanted me to come visit. He said it wouldn't be necessary. After all, we went months without seeing him when he was in Iraq. I was grateful because I wasn't sure I could bear visiting my son in jail. Being locked up always horrified me. I hate the thought of being behind bars with hard men doing hard time for living selfishly and violently, many having given up on a future, taking what they can get from 'right now'. I don't even like prison movies. I saw Shawshank Redemption. It was good. But I hated it.

Somehow I think I should have a deeper emotional response to this latest development. It's more alcoholic stupidity. A theft, a lost job, lost pay, an arrest, months in the court system, and now jail time. Shouldn't I be feeling something more intensely? Shouldn't Jody and I be crying, and crying out in humiliation and desperation?

Nothing. Numb. A case of 'I never thought it would come to this' only this time there have been too many others, so the feelings stay quiet, like a dying man too weak to move. And I try to remember the empty canvas and the world of promise. Maybe this will be the breakthrough...or maybe not.

I heard a preacher say that God sees the end from the beginning. That means Father always sees the dreams yet to be dreamed, and the hopes becoming reality. He never goes through the dark caverns of uncertainty or the valleys of doubt. Which is why, I suppose, that Christ needed to hang on the cross and shout to the empty sky, "why have you forsaken me." It was so I couldn't say that God was unwilling to live my doubts, and die my fears. He did both, and He did it willingly so He could settle the matter of empathy. He does know what it's like. But He knows the end from the beginning, too, which I do not know. To hang on to the unfulfilled dreams, I have to trust Him a while longer.

And that's another reason I was glad Ben told me I didn't need to come to the justice center to visit. The last time I looked at his face behind clear plastic was in that bassinette. I need to keep seeing him there in the upstairs hallway—to keep the hopes and dreams alive.

(24) IDOLS

The phone rings. I answer: "Hello?"

"Hey..." It is Ben. His voice is colorless, without expression. He is calling from a rehab facility in Los Angeles. Having exhausted every VA sponsored program in our region he has opted for a program in Southern California; a place recommended by a friend and advocate, a college professor and sociologist. As usual, Ben sees the shortcomings of the program. It is like a prison. They are doing it all wrong and he is being swept along in the current of incompetence; being forced to endure a system fraught with inadequacy, and he alone seems to be the only one who sees the truth, or is smart enough to see it.

So, he is depressed.

We talk for a time. He, about the weaknesses of the program, and I about the importance of hanging in there; about holding out for the elusive 90 days of sobriety that the experts say is the benchmark to strive for if there is to be hope for success. I tell him that if he thinks the program is flawed he still needs to see it through so he can make some constructive contributions later, when he's earned the right to be heard.

He complains that the program has made a Bible out of AA's "Big Book." He is appalled that some of the other patients—inmates—in the program are creating a "higher power" with convenient attributes. At one level, I'm pleased that he seems willing to defend the God of his heritage. But I know that he is a long way from surrender. He has had an intellectual understanding of God for many years, but yielding to him as a son has not been something he has chosen to do.

Ben says, "One of the guy's higher power is gonna help him stay sober so he can go into strip clubs without drinking!"

I agree that seems silly; self serving; a convenient deity; a god made to personal specifications.

After the conversation ends I think about my own convenient higher powers. I remember a day when I was out walking and praying. I had begun to quietly sing some songs and hymns as I walked along—careless, unfocused worship. I remember hearing myself sing, "have thine own way, Lord. Have thine own way. *I am the potter, thou art the clay..."* I stopped short when I realized what I had said; how I had rewritten the hymn and made myself the creator of God. I chuckled at first, but then choked a bit at the thought of how often, in practice, I made God in my own image. "Do as I say, Lord. Do as I say. I am the potter. Thou art the clay..."

How I wish I could impose my will on God! How I imagine I can! Lord, make Ben stop drinking. Make him turn to you. Make him behave himself and become the son we always hoped—prayed—he would be. Lord, make this nightmare stop. Lord, do as I say. Overcome Ben's will and sweep him helplessly into the kingdom and insist he be born again.

Do as I say, Lord...

My own prayers betray me. I have created a higher power that suits me, but who is not my Father. I have created an idol that does not hear. My heavenly Father is not inclined to overcome the will of his children. He insists that his children choose to hear Him, obey Him, and follow Him. He invites them to love Him and be changed. C.S. Lewis explained it in The Screwtape Letters: the Father wants people...

...whose life, on its miniature scale, will be qualitatively like His own...because their wills freely conform to His...He wants servants who can finally become sons...a world full of beings united to Him but still distinct...He cannot ravish. He can only woo...[they] are to be one with Him, but yet themselves. [1]

I know that is how God is. He has always given his creatures the choice. That was His choice. It was a decision He was willing to live with because, in the end, the result would be love, freely given and joyfully received. The god I would create, if it weren't an impotent idol, would be a tyrant and I would have, not a son, but a servant.

The price for the arrangement that God has chosen is high. It means that the ones He loves—that we love—are free to play the prodigal, to stumble repeatedly into pain and pointlessness.

A few weeks after the phone conversation about the weaknesses of the program Jody and I had taken a few days at the Oregon coast—a mini vacation. It was there that we got a text message from Ben's girlfriend. Had we heard from him? No. We thought he was safely in treatment. Apparently, not. She had received some enigmatic voicemails and text messages. After two months of a year-long program Ben had left LA. He was headed toward home. We packed up and prepared to intercept him there; to face whatever storm clouds might be brewing.

---

1 C.S. Lewis, The Screwtape Letters. (New York: Macmillan, 1975), p. 38

(25) DESPAIR

The strength of the burden bearers is failing
Yet there is much rubbish
And we ourselves are unable to build the wall
~Nehemiah 4:10)

The binge drinking—benders, they're called—has increased. He cuts himself. His friends drift away, except those who are willing to go with him to "party," Army buddies who, like Ben, measure their manhood by the quart—guns, war, and alcohol, the marks of strength and masculinity.

So, why is he at our house again? After so many failed attempts at helping him out of the whirlpit of drunken despair, what made us think this time would be different?

Hope, that fragile butterfly.

He had gone to the VA hospital for help, showed them the deep gashes he had gouged into his legs above the ankle; reported depression and passing blood when he went to the bathroom. They inspected the legs and pronounced that they were healing well, and asked him to produce a stool sample, which, after three days of drinking and little or no food, was not available. So, they released him. Sent him home.

Next patient, please…

He arrived home drunk. He confessed to the cutting and the fear that his body was breaking down under the relentless torrent of alcohol. He had apparently come to that all-important first step of AA's twelve: "We admitted we were powerless over alcohol - that our lives had become unmanageable." He said he needed to find in-patient treatment, long-term.

So, I begin—again—to try to seize the moment, to help him sort out his options and get him into treatment—ASAP. He can't go back to the house he shares with some drinking buddies and his ex-girlfriend whose manipulative behaviors never fail to trigger another bender. Other old roommates are either married, or have moved out of the area. One, another combat vet, is dead from an overdose of methadone.

"You can stay here," I tell him, "temporarily, until you can get into a treatment program." But treatment programs have waiting lists and every day spent waiting is 36 hours long. Plenty long enough to slip out of the house to 7-11 and score two more 40 ounce Pabst Blue Ribbon and a bottle of cheap wine—nearly a gallon of alcohol—drink it and be found in the morning on the basement floor. Ample time to come home in drunken despair and threaten to fight me for the right to go out for another drink. More than enough time for me to spend hours talking him down from another binge while he pours out endless confessions of his worthlessness and earnest assurances that we are good parents and that I, his father, am his hero.

And I, the impotent hero, try to keep him sober and safe (once, after letting him leave drunk he was hit by a car, breaking his leg and racking up a $30,000 uninsured medical bill). So, we wait together for the elusive "treatment" program. All the while I wonder how it is that I, the hero, was never trusted by the one who claims to admire me. I remember teaching him to swim. He flailed and struggled, unwilling to believe that I would never drop him. That is a metaphor for

Benjamin and me. All along the road to adulthood he has turned away, fought instruction, spurned example, insisted on his own way, resisted and rejected all others. Why would he rather believe that he is worthless and without hope, when I so heroically assured him that he has what it takes? And I believe that. Every word. But it is not enough that I believe, he must believe it, and he does not. He has trained himself to believe the truth as he sees it, even though it is a lie.

A few days ago Ben admitted that when he passed the self-proclaimed "homeless vet" standing at the freeway ramp with a cardboard sign he feared he was close to that destiny. He is right. He is not far from it. He could easily find himself standing alongside numberless prodigal sons just living the lie. There at the on-ramp they stand. The world flows by avoiding the glance of the old man—fearfully old, hopelessly old, alcohol old—standing at the wrong end of the rainbow with a cardboard sign: anything helps...God bless...

But the truth is, sometimes nothing helps and God's blessings, like wrapped packages, remain unopened. Sometimes, people would rather live a lie than a dream; rather lie down than fly.

Against such ruthless truth my only defense is tears. My only comfort is that, once again, my own pain opens a window on the heart of God. Of his own prodigal child he said,

When Israel was young, I loved him. Out of Egypt I called my son. The more I called, the more he went away...

God's love contains the world and all of its wonderful potential. His heart breaks at its desperation and its hopelessness. If I have learned anything from my son it is this: God's earnest desires for me are true. My fear and self-loathing are the lies. Yet, how often do I choose to lie down among the stones rather than believe the truth of God and let hope take wing like a butterfly?

How often do you?

The epiphany of Wendell Berry's fictional barber, Jayber Crow rings true: "If God loved the world even before the event at Bethlehem, that meant He loved it as it was, with all its faults. That would be Hell itself, in part. He would be like a father with a wayward child, whom He can't help and can't forget."

So it is with fathers and sons. Whether love contains the whole world or a single child, it bears all things, believes all things, hopes all things, endures all things. Love never ends, even though there are times it wishes it could.

(26) GRACE UPON GRACE

I am driving over the bridge, heading south to seek after the welfare of my son who has not called to confirm when and where I should pick him up. There will be 45 minutes of driving and I don't know what to expect when I arrive. Has he lost his phone? Has he overslept? Was he out drinking again? Is that why he didn't answer or return our call?

And then the fear finds its mark, shoved up under my ribs like a spear. What if...

Suddenly, I know how the story ends. It ends as I make my way cautiously down the stairs into the rubble of his basement "apartment." I gasp as I see the silhouetted form of my son hanging from the rafters. I imagine untying him and lowering his body, stiff in death, to the floor and kneeling there wailing desperately, trying to gulp some life for myself from the atmosphere of death all around.

It ends in the bathtub, his scarlet life, poured down the drain and me trying to decide how I will tell his mother. It ends with a gunshot. It ends with an overdose of pills.

Who will do the funeral? Me? I have done the memorial for my father, my mother, my nephew. I have officiated at scores of funerals. Can I do the memorial service for my own son? I stand before a church filled with family. I see the faces of those who we love and have loved us through the trials of

101

this life. I see the faces of my son's friends, not a few of them accomplices to his destruction—I detest them.

Mile after mile I pray for the images to stop. I force my mind over the prison walls of fear, into some other place, and each time it is dragged back to the dark terror of what may await me.

I park the car in the driveway. My heart is pounding; breathing shallow. I rest my head and hands on the steering wheel and pray, "God help me. Please help me get through this." I knock on the door...

And then he is standing in the open doorway, glassy-eyed from last night's drinking, but alive. He is alive. I reach out and lock my arms around him, weeping on his neck, as the fear evaporates and hope, once again, emerges. Weak, I sit on the couch, shocked at the depth of my own feeling—a little embarrassed.

A turning point. An outpouring of such love would surely be the moment of breakthrough that would turn his heart toward those who love him and cause him to strive for freedom and wholeness. Surely, his life would change. How could he resist the passion of his father's love?

Yet, the ugly spiral continues. The butterflies continue to die among the stones. With each one, my heart has grown weaker. The strength to grasp the hope ebbs.

I see less of the man I dreamed he would become and more of the one he seems determined to be. He seems to have set out with deliberateness to be everything I have always hated about disfigured manhood.

Drinking. Smoking. Partying. Gambling. Foul-mouthed. Unkind. Selfish. Abusive. Mocking. Smelling of smoke and alcohol. At home in rancid taverns and among reprobates and miscreants.

I detest it. All of it. That I should be the father of such a one is hardly bearable. I wish I could forget him. Reclaim my life and put this interminable season of reckless debauchery behind me. To forget the lies; the times when my affection only made me feel foolish when it was repaid only with more of the same; to sleep through the night without fear and dread; to turn away one last time and be free of love.

When the Creator of this world looks upon it sinking into depravity—when He sees the hatred and the filth; the malice and the cruelty; the selfishness and the violence, when He sees all that He hates, will He turn away?

No. Because the love of the Father in heaven exceeds my feeble love. He has already turned His face away from all that, when He turned away from Christ on the cross. It had to be a cross. Anything less brutal could never stand amidst the refuse of human depravity and declare it forgiven. Atonement for the sins of the world—all that the Creator detests in His children—had to be the cross.

And that is what makes Him Father. Grace beyond limits. Forgiveness without end. Hope beyond endurance. Life to overcome death. That is grace. It is the love that never fails and will prevail in spite of all that is detestable among His children.

(27) LOSS

It dawned on me the other day that I've stopped talking to Ben when he's not around. It seems I have come to the conclusion that, even in my imagined conversations with him, he is not listening.

Am I losing—have I lost—hope? Maybe. After all the years of struggle and desperate optimism, perhaps my heart has decided to face the facts: the prodigal is not coming home. He is content to remain in the far country squandering what remains after he has lost everything.

I remember when it happened. It was during a prayer time, kneeling in my office. My mind dropped away from prayer and slipped into a place I didn't want to go. It was the place of lost things—the world of what could have been; ought to have been. It was a melancholy place of grief where I mourned the losses of the past 15 years. The high school dances that Ben did not attend. The cars he never drove. The sports he never played, the awards he never got, the degree he never earned, and the compliments he never received.

The pride I never felt.

I began to weep when I thought of the daughter-in-law I did not have. She was pretty and had a ready smile. She loved being outdoors and had a sense of humor that matched her husband's. She was smart and felt like one of the family. Jody and I had loved her from the moment we met her. Ben had chosen wisely as his sisters had when they found their husbands.

I thought about my grandchildren who had not been born, cousins to my other grandchildren who I nicknamed, 'Tin-ribs' and 'Buckshot'; 'Fastball' and 'Sunbeam.' These were the kids that never got their own nicknames because I never knew them.

I found myself in a cloud of sorrow; half ashamed that I had allowed it to sweep over me, but somehow wanting to admit the pain of it. I know it was maudlin and self-indulgent, but I felt entitled. I felt I had earned a private moment of unguarded honesty. The images that I indulged that morning were, after all, my legacy. They were the reward for being a good father and they had never been allowed to exist. All the good that I had imagined for my son had been rejected, traded away for a bucket of swill.

They say that letting go is one of the purposes of grief, a necessary step toward laying aside what cannot be changed so that life can continue. As I consider that thought, I realize that even God sometimes has to let go. Jesus sat overlooking Jerusalem (for so I imagine the scene) weeping. He said, *"Jerusalem! Jerusalem! How often I would have gathered you as a hen gathers her chicks, yet you wouldn't have it! Behold your house has been left to you desolate..."*

Wasn't that despair pouring from the heart of God? Wasn't that a torrent of grief over what had not been—would never be? Even the heavenly Father, the eternal fountain of love, comes to an end-point, weeping, crying out to His prodigal creations, "Very well, then. Let it be done according to your will."

That morning, without really intending to, I had admitted that love, no matter how tenacious and determined, can be a force too weak to save the life of one who refuses it. I found myself wallowing somewhere between numbness and resignation; between steadfastness and 'so be it.'

Even the Father who is God, must, at times, let go. He cannot do it easily—certainly not willingly—but eventually he let's go. And in the letting go there is crucifixion.

(28) ADDICTION

He stood by his car and smoked a cigarette. Then he got in, drove away and was gone. His departure had been a week in the making. It was supposed to have taken place seven days before, but he had only managed to move as far as the driveway, sleeping in his car for a few of those days. The rest he spent on the foam rubber pad on the basement floor where he had been for two months.

He had left the last rehab program and predictably, landed back home; and just as predictably we had opened the door to him. Once again we had taken the chrysalis in our hands and attempted to protect it through the long awaited metamorphosis. And once again, we found ourselves among the stones when he slipped away alone to a nearby tavern or to meet a friend for more than a few drinks. The triggers to his drinking were always mysterious and unpredictable. Most disturbing, they were persistent.

It was all too clear that our efforts to help were fruitless. We were not helping him. We were becoming—had become— like a gambler staying in the game hoping to recoup his losses. When our son finally stepped into sobriety and wholeness, wWe would be vindicated for all the times we reached out to him. But the more we played the game the more we looked like chumps. The more we looked like…

Enabler.

The dreaded label—the scarlet letter—worn by so many hapless parents and spouses who won't recognize the truth. It is the word that is used to describe a person who makes it possible for someone to persist in self-destructive behavior by helping them avoid the consequences. We were being forced to recognize it in ourselves and we knew it had to stop. We told him that he had to leave. He could no longer live under our roof.

The ultimatum seemed to find its mark. He did not disagree with our decision, not that he ever did, but this time it seemed different, more final. Moreover, he was nearly broke. He had already spent most of his government check on alcohol so he could not even afford a cheap Motel. He started looking around for friends who could put him up for a few days. Nobody would. The long spiral of addiction had taken its toll on his relationships.

He did what he always did when facing an intractable problem: he drank, spending the last few dollars he had. Then he slept in his car in our driveway. When the temperature was forecast to drop into the 20s we brought him inside, always reminding him that we were not going to change our minds; he could not stay.

Then the first of the month came and more money appeared in his account. He moved out; threw some of his belongings into a suitcase and checked into a motel.

In the silence of the house after he left I considered what had happened. He was alone—an alcoholic by himself is in bad company. It was Saturday night. It was the first of the month so he had money. Nothing was standing in the way of another binge but his own self-control. Disaster. Failure. All of the conditions were in place. I wondered if he should have stayed a few more days. I wished he had non-drinking friends.

I worried about how he would make it through the night. I wondered what he would do. I prayed. I texted an interested friend and told him what had happened. I prayed some more. For a moment, I considered calling an old friend of Ben's who did not drink and suggest he call...

Suddenly, I realized the truth. I was in the habit of helping my son. I imagined myself to be his only hope. I was going through withdrawal. I was an addict.

"Let go and let God" is the oft-repeated aphorism. It is embossed on stationary, painted on T-shirts, embroidered, recited, memorized, and nearly canonized. Yet, before that quiet moment in the living room it had never been realized, at least not by me.

Let go. Let God. Dig in. Cry out. Trust. Remember that God is my Father and Ben's. Only God's love is pure. Mine is a weak reflection, and worse, when allowed to become desperate it is tainted with pride and selfishness. It becomes lofty in its conceit, claiming that it is the only hope.

There was a day when Jesus came upon a certain father who cried out to Him, *"Lord, have mercy on my son, for he ... suffers terribly. He often falls into the fire, and often into the water."* [1] The father knew he could not help his son so he had stopped trying. He had reached the limits of his own love, so he gave his son to Jesus whose love had no limits. I had to do the same. .

---

1 Mat 17:14-15 (ESV)

(29) WOUNDS

While he was a long way off, his father saw him
and felt compassion for him,
and ran and embraced him and kissed him...

~From the story of the Prodigal Son

"What happened to your arm?"

It's a question that I get asked occasionally. There is a scar across my right elbow where I tried to chop off my arm with a gas-powered pruning saw. The accident happened over thirty years ago. When I am asked about the scar, I tell about the wound, and I remember that I would give that arm for the life of my children.

Wounds tell stories. I suppose that is why I felt compelled to share this one. Is the story merely cathartic? Is it self-pity or self-justifying? The Lord knows I've pondered those questions. I think in the telling of this prodigal journey it is my way of shouting that I will not give up. I refuse to amputate hope. I will hold on to it as though it were a promise. I will not let wounds bleed, but offer them to my Father and ask Him to heal them, and trust that Ben's wounds will likewise become scars of victory.

In Christ's body after the resurrection, wounds told of redemption and eternal life. Jesus, the suffering servant, carried away the sins of the world—His generation, the generations before, and the sins of the generations to come. He took the wounds in His body and unleashed a tidal wave of reconciliation that was to rush upon the human race and pour out across the millennia to touch even us.

But why did Jesus have to carry the wounds of crucifixion even after His resurrection? Surely a resurrected body could have been a perfect, unscarred body. Why the open wounds? Because they were the evidence. They proved that life had been poured out. They proved brokenness is the cost of healing. His eternal, resurrected body bore the marks of the horror of sin in order to prove that sin and rebellion cannot be undone but can be forgiven—horribly, passionately, and continually forgiven. That's why Wendell Berry's thoughts carry so much weight. Indeed, God is the Father who knows...

..the wayward child and the course of its waywardness and its suffering. That His love contains all the world does not show that the world does not matter, or that He and we do not suffer it unto death; it shows that the world is Hell only in part. But His love can contain it only by compassion and mercy, which, if not Hell entirely, would be at least a crucifixion.

The reality of the prodigal journey is that the prodigal does not wander alone. His family and friends travel with him, bound to him and dragged along by chains of love. From this, comes the most important lesson of all. If my heart aches at my son's emptiness; shudders at his foolishness; fears for his recklessness; weeps for his lostness, then is not that the evidence that my heavenly Father also feels these things for me—for all of us?

We have experienced wounds together, Benjamin and I, the ones we have received and the ones we inflicted. But Jesus experienced them long before we did. At the end of the journey we will find that our heavenly Father will heal our wounds because His Son carried them for us. That is the message of the Eucharist—communion, the "good gift." In it we see Jesus, pierced through and crushed. We say, "our Lord and our God!" as we look upon the living One—his shattered hands and feet, His pierced side. The wounds prove that the work of Christ goes on. Jesus' wounds should have been lethal, but they were merely mortal. Their presence bore witness to the miracle of resurrection life. He carried His wounds so we could be assured that ours can heal.

What frightens me is the knowledge that we must choose healing. Like the son in Jesus' story we must come to our senses and come home. That is what I am waiting for, hoping for, praying for. Such is the love of the Father. It is His legacy of love passed down to earthly fathers—a candle to the furnace of His own passion, but still fierce and sacrificial. It yearns; it relentlessly draws water from the well of expectancy, anticipating the day when we...

> Welcome the traveler home
> As out in this wide world
> We wander alone
> Though our ways twist and bend
> We know in the end
> We will welcome the traveler home
>
> Though late is the hour
> And long is the road from the path I have known
> But for this prodigal son
> The long journey's done
> When you welcome the traveler home.

ABOUT THE AUTHOR

Dan Mayhew lives in Portland, OR. He has been married to his wife, Jody, for 40 years and has three grown children and five grandchildren. He is a former high school teacher, a minister and a writer. Dan writes from a Christian perspective on matters of faith and spiritual life. He has also been a humor columnist and publishes his comic work as Dan "Max" Mayhew.

You may contact him at
wings@stonebutterfly.net

His websites are

http://stonebutterfly.net
http://tween2worlds.us

8260675R0

Made in the USA
Charleston, SC
23 May 2011